WHAT YOUR COLLEAGUES ARE SAYING . . .

Fullan and Quinn make the case for an educational paradigm that places humanity and its needs at the center. In clear and compelling language, they explain how we can move quickly from the schools we have to the ones our society needs. For those who recognize that education is critical to creating a more just and equitable future, this book will serve as a guide and source of inspiration.

—Pedro Noguera, Dean
Rossier School of Education,
University of Southern California
Los Angeles, California

The Drivers is truly a book for the moment. Fullan and Quinn offer a set of interlocking design principles, brought to life by cases of school- and district-level transformation, which light a way toward a future where all can thrive. The book manages to be both clear-eyed and aspirational—a combination that will resonate with stakeholders at all levels of the system.

—Sarah Fine, Director
San Diego Teacher Residency,
High Tech High Graduate School of Education
San Diego, California

This book is an engaging must-read for all educators involved in systems change because it offers strategies centered on the humanity and well-being of stakeholders. It will help you rebuild a framework around systems change with meaningful insights from successful school communities around the world.

—Michele Broadnax, President and CEO
Los Angeles Education Partnership
Los Angeles, California

Fullan and Quinn have braided together some of the most important, current, and cutting-edge research with a clear understanding of the challenges of moving theory to practice. This book offers powerful advice on shifts that must happen in our school system and society if we are ever to achieve the pluralistic, multiracial democracy we have promised to our children.

—Jeff Duncan-Andrade, Professor
Latina/o Studies & Race and Resistance Studies
San Francisco State University
San Francisco, California

A timely book that provides an innovative approach to education. Fullan and Quinn draw on extensive international and practical experience to comprehensively understand the drivers essential for fostering change in education. This is a must-read for educators, policy makers, and anyone interested in positively impacting education and the world.

—Leandro Folgar Ruétalo, Presidente
Ceibal
Uruguay

This is truly great work—an arresting and compelling guide to transforming our systems of education. It demands the exercise of our crucial role as stewards in service to and in cooperation with others. *The Drivers* reactivates the lifeblood of a human system of learning.

—Anthony Mackay, Board Co-Chair
National Center on Education & the Economy
Washington, D.C.

Fullan and Quinn's passionate and easy-to-read book is a call to action that will inspire and inform those seeking to transform our education system so that every learner has the deep learning required to survive and thrive in a complex world. This is what is needed to drive the necessary transformation of our schools.

—Sandra Milligan, Director and Enterprise Professor
Assessment Research Center,
Melbourne Graduate School of Education
Melbourne, Australia

Fullan and Quinn's four interrelated drivers build an ecosystem that enables learners to live with themselves, live with people who are different from them, and live with the planet. This is the daring and ambitious agenda we need given the challenges humanity faces.

—Andreas Schleicher, Director
Directorate of Education and Skills, OECD
France

THE
DRIVERS

THE
DRIVERS

TRANSFORMING LEARNING FOR STUDENTS, SCHOOLS, AND SYSTEMS

MICHAEL FULLAN
JOANNE QUINN

CORWIN

CORWIN
A Sage Company

FOR INFORMATION:

Corwin

A SAGE Company

2455 Teller Road

Thousand Oaks, California 91320

(800) 233-9936

www.corwin.com

SAGE Publications Ltd.

1 Oliver's Yard

55 City Road

London EC1Y 1SP

United Kingdom

SAGE Publications India Pvt. Ltd.

Unit No 323-333, Third Floor, F-Block

International Trade Tower Nehru Place

New Delhi 110 019

India

SAGE Publications Asia-Pacific Pte. Ltd.

18 Cross Street #10-10/11/12

China Square Central

Singapore 048423

Vice President and
Editorial Director: Monica Eckman

Senior Acquisitions Editor: Tanya Ghans

Content Development
Manager: Desirée A. Bartlett

Senior Editorial Assistant: Nyle De Leon

Production Editor: Melanie Birdsall

Copy Editor: Heather Kerrigan

Typesetter: C&M Digitals (P) Ltd.

Proofreader: Jeff Bryant

Cover Designer: Gail Buschman

Marketing Manager: Morgan Fox

Printed in Canada

Library of Congress Cataloging-in-Publication Data

Names: Fullan, Michael, author. | Quinn, Joanne, author.

Title: The drivers : transforming learning for students, schools, and systems / Michael Fullan, Joanne Quinn.

Description: Thousand Oaks, California : Corwin, 2024. | Includes bibliographical references and index.

Identifiers: LCCN 2023015713 | ISBN 9781071855010 (paperback) | ISBN 9781071922088 (epub) | ISBN 9781071922071 (epub) | ISBN 9781071922064 (pdf)

Subjects: LCSH: Educational change—United States. | Holistic education—United States. | Education—Aims and objectives—United States.

Classification: LCC LA217.2 .F866 2024 | DDC 370.11—dc23/eng/20230505

LC record available at https://lccn.loc.gov/2023015713

This book is printed on acid-free paper.

MIX
Paper from
responsible sources
FSC® C103567
www.fsc.org

23 24 25 26 27 10 9 8 7 6 5 4 3 2 1

Contents

Preface

O ver the past half century, we have worked to help develop education as a vehicle for transforming society and its relationship to the planet. Increasingly we have been drawn to work with practitioners of all ages, especially the very young, but really everyone. We have come to have close relationships "through the doing"—with students and communities, schools, districts, states, provinces, and countries around the world.

We have seen inspiring ad hoc examples of what can go right, but the overall societal trend is markedly less and less favorable. For the first time ever, increasing numbers of people, especially the all-important young, know that the collapse of society is a distinct possibility. Global society and its subparts have become incredibly complex, and thus extremely challenging to manage. But there is a variable that could make a huge difference: how consciously humans begin to affect the future. We know that a system solution (and that indeed is what it will take) is incredibly complex. We also know, thanks to recent work in the past decade, what such a system solution might look like. The main goal of this book is to flesh out and capture what this new model of action looks like and how it operates to generate new results.

We think of the new model as fundamentally based on the humanity paradigm that values all living things on the planet—their survival and flourishing. This is in contrast to what we might call the laissez-faire paradigm, which has governed our evolution to this point in history (see Figure 0.1). The laissez-faire paradigm essentially lets things be until they become so problematic that action becomes essential. It is like living life through the rearview mirror. Laissez-faire allows, and one could say enables, self-interest. The humanity paradigm seeks the individual and the common good as they enable each other. Perhaps the laissez-faire model was understandable when no one was paying attention and the problems were not so severe. Today, standing by while the universe deteriorates is inexcusable. Read this book, learn from our vignettes, join with others, and pursue the humanity paradigm—*as if your life depends on it!* Because it probably does.

FIGURE 0.1 ● The Battle of the Paradigms

Image source: pixabay.com/openclipart-vectors

The core premise of the humanity paradigm is based on values and actions that enable all living things to cope, survive, develop, and flourish under the complex conditions of this century. The humanity paradigm centers on *the ability to learn how to learn, know oneself, and care about the other, and the environment, and to do all of this in concert with others.*

> *The humanity paradigm centers on* the ability to learn how to learn, know oneself, and care about the other, and the environment, and to do all of this in concert with others.

In the course of our work, we have identified four drivers that in effect constitute the engine of the model. A driver is a force and set of actions that propel the system forward. The interrelated set of drivers are Well-Being and Learning, Social and Machine Intelligence, Equity-Equality Investments, and Systemness. Together they are the means to fulfilling the goal of human flourishing for all.

We introduce these drivers in Chapter 1 and provide detailed vignettes of how they work in action in Chapters 2 through 5. We will also feature the concept of coherence making, which is a critical component of any solution (Fullan & Quinn, 2016). Coherence has two distinctive features: it is *subjective* and it must be *shared*. The standard to be met is to accomplish "the shared depth of understanding about the nature of the work and of any *solutions!*" Such understanding was difficult in 2016 when we published *Coherence*. Today, it is incredibly more challenging where the depth and complexity of the problems have never before been faced by humankind. Many of the solutions are unknown. They must be discovered and developed in the heat of the moment. And very little is static. New problems emerge, solutions yield to exhaustion, turnover is at an all-time high, and what works in one situation may not be applicable to another. Progress at times may seem near impossible.

The expansion of the humanity paradigm is that more and more of us see ourselves and our collectivities—our very humanity at its best—as the only way forward. The four drivers working in concert is our future.

In 2023 and beyond, what we do as humans will make a world of difference. In the past, leaders were more distant from the general population. In contrast, in the present era we are all being called on to step in and save the present while we create a better future. The expansion of the humanity paradigm is that more and more of us see ourselves and our collectivities—our very humanity at its best—as the only way forward. The four drivers working in concert is our future.

The drivers are intrinsically interrelated—within a given driver, and across all four. Thus, well-being and learning must feed each other. Without this reciprocity it might be possible to focus on well-being without linking it to learning. One can become immersed in social learning (collaboration), seeing machine intelligence as dangerous, thereby failing to figure out how to leverage artificial intelligence (AI). We can get lost in the miasma of siloed equity and equality without advancing either. Systemness, a new concept, can remain at the abstract level instead of becoming a meaningful opportunity to see the world differently and act accordingly.

By the same token, it is essential to see the four drivers as feeding each other and being fed by the others. We are talking about a synergistic solution that can become the underpinning of a new Well-Being and Learning system for all—one that can both save the planet and enable humanity to thrive. The good news is that some of us are discovering how to do this (see our five detailed vignettes). The better news is that as people do this new work, they want to share it in real time—partly because they realize that if others don't get better, we will all suffer (maybe to extinction), and partly because they truly want to help others and get feedback that will strengthen their own efforts. The even better news is that it is the young (including the very young) often get it first and lead the way by example.

This book builds on our previous work—*Coherence* (2016), *Nuance* (2019), *Spirit Work* (2022), *Deep Learning* (2018, 2020)—but is more systematic in that here we provide a complete model linked to action. Because it is complete it will benefit all audiences associated with individual and system development. In many ways, the model has been developed with our global partners in the field. The model needs to be formulated and tested more fully. We hope our book will feed into this domain of helping the humanity paradigm become established as a beacon to transforming the world of human development.

Almost 2,000 years ago, Roman emperor and philosopher Marcus Aurelius said, "It is not death that [man] should fear, but [he] should fear never beginning to live." This is an exciting (and dangerous) time to live. The inventions and dynamics, both on and off the planet, in the current age are both magnificent and horrific. Having a chance to sort out this mess and its underlying treasures in real time in this decade and beyond is about as human as you can get. In previous generations, the majority of humans were assigned fixed positions in life, many of which were "nasty, brutish, and short" as philosopher Thomas Hobbes observed in 1651. As the vignettes in this book reveal, we can now realistically identify what's worth fighting for and certain pathways to get there. No guarantees, but definitely the way to live: After all, there are only seventy-seven years left in the current century. We have a lofty goal for this book. Our main goal is to move from a discussion of what is wrong to a grounded actionable framework that could help change the odds in favor of deep and continuous transformation—transformation is the concept—mere improvement will not be sufficient.

We love the intrigue of the observation made by evolutionary biologist E. O. Wilson (2017):

> Science owns the warrant to explore everything deemed factual and possible, but the humanities borne aloft by both fact and fantasy, have the power of everything not only possible but conceivable. (p. 70)

The humanity paradigm has such unknown limits. We sense the magic that young people can generate in the next period if we help and enable them. We also feel the anxiety and doubt that people of all ages express. It is the case that there were relentless reasons from 2020 to 2022 for humanity to become deeply discouraged and overwhelmed. The reader will see in our arguments and vignettes that the concern of despair can be a step on the way to new success. We have to be equipped with some powerful ideas (we call them drivers) and with the power of collaboration in order to turn the current tide. There is another concept that we find essential for complex times and that is *nuance*. Nuance concerns shades of meaning, especially concerning anything complex. Our book is about increasing capacity for nuance—build your nuance by understanding what we will describe as the humanity paradigm. Lose your nuance and you lose your humanity.

We will provide new evidence, new individual and collective reasons, and specific strategies to be hopeful about the next twenty-five years and more. In the beginning, we name it *learned hopefulness*. Once you make some progress and feel the momentum (as do those in the vignettes we present), push harder and deeper and call it *transformation!* As indicated, we have been working on a promising solution to enacting the drivers to foster the human paradigm. We call this integrated approach *Deep Learning*. It impacts well-being, learning, and equity by creating learning experiences for students to develop the Global Competencies they will need to flourish in a complex world. These 6Cs are character/compassion, citizenship, collaboration, communication, creativity, and critical thinking. Deep Learning is defined as the process of developing these six Global Competencies. We will present several vignettes illustrating ways that systems are using the drivers to forge a new purpose and process for learning. To get to Deep Learning, *systems must change* their very foundations, structures, and cultures.

Even in the positive cases, we recognize that our current examples represent a minuscule (although varied) part of the world. But if we can show progress in sizable systems, and identify the reasons why, we may be on to something. Success can spread rapidly when current conditions become bad enough, combined with clear examples of success in comparable circumstances. Go slow to go fast, as we say. In this book, there are five vignettes across the four drivers. Each one is substantial. We suggest that you consider the most relevant cases to your situation and delve into them more deeply.

Success can spread rapidly when current conditions become bad enough, combined with clear examples of success in comparable circumstances.

Although our knowledge has developed more in Western countries, we are working actively in several countries in Latin America and the Asia Pacific region. Contextual literacy (knowing and caring about the culture you are in) is a requirement when you apply the ideas that we present. Our aim is to move the purpose of education away from its 200-year yolk to the status quo, toward a system that is laced with qualities of constant evolutionary renewal—a force that continually integrates genes, culture, and consciousness. This book is about the struggle between proactive humanity and the laissez-faire drift that has been allowed to unfold thus far.

We end with a crucial point: *No one driver will be effective in the absence of one or more of the other three.* After all, we are dealing with *system change!* Remember this when you are dealing with any one driver. When taking up each driver, ask yourself: *What is the role of each of the other three, and the four in concert?*

Our book represents an ambitious agenda out of necessity.

We can almost taste a new beginning, among the young, but also across various sectors of what could become powerful "virtuous cascades" (to use Homer-Dixon's [2020] hopeful phrase). The drivers and our underlying Deep Learning model are one such attempt. We can think of no better way to spend our individual and collective time in the coming decade.

. . . .

CHAPTER 1

Where to From Here?

Our concern is to press into the future. We set the stage by considering the state of education as it evolved from the past century to 2019 (pre-COVID), then we characterize the COVID-19 period (2020 to 2022+), and finally take up the future (2023 onward) using this as an opportunity to position the drivers and associated Deep Learning. The focus of our book is on education. But because we seek system transformation, we need to call on other key sectors, namely the economy (especially poverty), social conditions (especially distrust), and climate (especially collapse). Despite the Western bias of our database, the themes have relevance for all parts of the globe (and much of our work is now in those jurisdictions).

THE EVOLVING STATE OF EDUCATION

THE QUIET BUT DEADLY DECLINE (1950 TO 2019)

As a preteen and early teenager one of us lived through the golden decade of the 1950s in Canada, but the trends were similar in many Western countries. It was easy to be optimistic and not recognize the early signs of deterioration, best captured by Claudia Goldin and Lawrence Katz (2008) in their classic book *The Race Between Technology and Education.*

In brief, Golden and Katz found that high school graduation rates and social mobility increased after World War II until the late 1970s, and then declined steadily for the subsequent fifty years to the present.

In a mutual causal coupling, a second trend revealed a small percentage of capitalists who garnered larger and larger shares of the financial pie while everyone else declined in terms of mobility and wealth. The economists who reported these findings are Mariana Mazzucato (2018, 2021), Heather Boushey (2019), Stephanie Kelton (2020), Kate Raworth (2017), and Carla Mattei (2022). Together these authors describe in detail laissez-faire at its worst.

It takes a while for new insights to be widely appreciated, and even more so before many can act on them. Consider the trends—gross domestic product (GDP) is the traditional measure of system financial growth. In the United States between the end of WWII and the late 1970s, most people's quality of life grew in line with overall output growth. Then it changed dramatically as a function of a financial system in which the vast majority of GDP goes to capital (those who already hold money) compared to labor or "the people." Countless statistical analyses reveal these cumulative distortions. For example, from 1980 to 2007 the income share of the top 1% expanded from 9.4% to 22.6% of growth. Raworth (2017) documents the hollowing out of the middle class, where the gap between the poor and the middle class is now less than the gap between the middle and the top (both the middle and the lower descended as the very rich leaped ahead).

In a further study, economist Mattei (2022) shows how "the capital order" (favoring and enhancing the rich over the worker) was established and baked into the world system in the 1920s! Thus, our driver—equity and equality—is up against a formidable foe. We can, however, work forcefully on equity (fairer front-end investments) and equality (for the first time attempting to achieve equitable outcomes, as in the San Diego County vignette we present later). The silver lining may turn out to be the likelihood that equity and equality benefit all, while the opposite negatively affects all.

COVID-19 (2020 TO 2022+)

The questions we are asking now are: Will the pandemic result in a worse system? A chance to establish brand-new superior systems? Or will we see ad hoc tinkering and other forms of lurching in whichever direction? No one knows what is likely to happen. Our best bet is to focus on how we can use the opportunity to establish a clear and better purpose for developing society, along with a practical, deep, systematic set of drivers (a set of four interrelated action strategies focusing on changing the system itself) that could take us to a much better future. If there was ever a time to seize the moment, it is now.

Valerie Hannon and Julie Temperley (2022) brilliantly summarized ten shocks revealed by the pandemic (we include nine here, omitting the one on higher education).

THE PANDEMIC SHOCK

1. How enormously important the social function of schools was. On every survey about what (if anything) students missed about school the item that came top was—friends and people.

2. That, notwithstanding decades of expectation that digital technology would transform learning. When it came to it, almost all schools were woefully unprepared. Technology had not been brought into the DNA of schools, and the removal of face-to-face connection revealed how primitive the majority of use was.

3. That whilst some schools knew and understood their communities, it was revealed how many did not. The home circumstances and real-life conditions of their families came as a revelation to many schools.

(Continued)

(Continued)

4. How the flexibility of *release* from attendance at school had been enjoyed by students, especially those for whom the rigidities of factory-style school routines did not fit.

5. It was revealed how the functioning of economies depended on the safe custody of children to free up parents to work. Whilst home schooling was revealed as a viable and attractive option for some (a tiny minority), most parents needed others, elsewhere, to look after their children, even as working from home became normalised.

6. It was revealed how the standardized assessment industry consumes time, energy and money. And for what?

7. Leadership is a key determinant. Whether of countries, cities or the local primary school, leadership can make the difference: between optimism and hope; vitality or despair; and in the case of the health security of nations, literally between life and death.

8. The equity gap, which was already grotesque, is now unconscionable and unsustainable. Social safety nets were seen to be eroded or non-existent. Poverty and race were revealed to be pre-existing conditions for vulnerability—to viral infection and many other ills. Contrasts could not be ignored in the life circumstances of children—some of whom enjoyed rich, varied and enjoyable learning experiences during lockdown; whilst others had a full stop to their learning. Some endured increased levels of domestic violence towards both women and children.

9. The occasion of COVID-19 gave many people cause to reflect upon their values; up what *really* mattered. Care became priceless; oil became worthless. Nature blossomed and gave solace. Relationships were understood to be at the very essence of a good life.

Source: Hannon and Temperley (2022).

A darn good list, we say. Let's use it to draw conclusions about education at the end of 2022. Education has played three main roles since 1950 (and before): custodial, looking after young people while their parents worked, and perhaps teaching them how to get along with others; sorting, with respect to occupations and their related place in society; and academic achievement. All three roles have suffered body blows in the past seventy-five years, which have been substantially aggravated during COVID-19. The custodial role was never a happy one. Now with COVID many students feel less compelled to attend school regularly; many parents have become more forgiving about nonattendance, while for some students school is their safest place to be.

Analyzing the second role, sorting, reveals a job market in upheaval. Graduating from high school or college no longer guarantees securing full-time employment with a living wage. What to do remains a mystery for increasing numbers of students.

The third purpose, individual academic achievement—the bellwether of public schooling when we went to school—has lost credibility and relevance. In a policy report on right and wrong drivers, Fullan (2021) named "academic obsession" as the first wrong driver. Academic obsession—the preoccupation with testing, grades, getting into the best post-secondary institutions *at any cost*—has also ruined many a winner (one study called them the "wounded winners") as well as scores of losers (see Markovits, 2020; Sandel, 2020). Academic grades, per se, are *not an intrinsic motivator* for the majority of students! The content of academic learning by itself does not prepare one for life. The net effect of current outdated public education is that about 80% of secondary school students are either alienated or bored (Malin, 2018; Milligan, 2020).

Similarly, in the perspective of the past 100 years, sociologists Jal Mehta and Amanda Datnow (2020) conclude that there is a yawning gap in how schools are organized versus how youth learn.

What youth say they want are

- Opportunities to do work that has purpose and meaning
- Strong connections to adults and peers (relationships/belongingness)
- To be viewed in asset-based ways
- For their identities to be valued
- An opportunity to contribute to the world

To say that the current education system is no longer fit for purpose is a gross understatement! The need for a transformed system is evident. On the one hand, the pandemic has provided an opportunity to do just that—transform the system. But it has also presented some dilemmas. There is the tendency to jump on loss of learning as the priority, which by itself would be an effort to capture a bad past. Related, we all know that to a degree almost everyone is near exhaustion from the mental and physical drain of the past three years. The toll of this experience could be (or more accurately could be made to be) temporary *if* we could enable a new system that would be both worth fighting for and deeply energizing.

SHIFTING THE PARADIGM: A NEW PURPOSE FOR EDUCATION AND A NEW SET OF DRIVERS

The new purpose of education is: *To cultivate civic-minded changemakers who make a difference in their own lives and in society.* The framework and strategies for accomplishing the transformation from the present is the subject of the rest of this book. As we say, "Get good at learning, and good at life."

Thomas Kuhn (1962) in his classic book *The Structure of Scientific Revolutions,* warned us that it's going to be damn difficult to change any embedded paradigm (principles that govern models of thinking and action). Kuhn argues that it won't be sufficient even if the existing system is catastrophically ineffective. We also need an attractive alternative system to take its place. Because the new model, by definition, has not yet been proven, it cannot easily carry the day. Moreover, when a new model comes along it is easy to implement it superficially without realizing it (you don't know what you don't know, or one can only stand so much discomfort in learning the new way). This is a phenomenon that Fullan wrote about in a two-part *Education Week* op-ed focusing on the inhibitors, and enablers of system change (Fullan, 2023b). Our plan is to push the limits of possible system transformation at a time that furnishes the opportunity to engage in work so essential to the future of the planet. More than pushing the limits, we want to identify and help develop brand-new Well-Being and Learning models in action. These models are deeper, more comprehensive, and larger in scope than ever before.

To do this we offer a strong paradigm with strategies that guide the action; five vignettes from four different countries that show success in action. Our best evidence comes from working with practitioners (students, teachers, parents, administrators) who are leading the way, in word and deed, which means that they can talk the walk, and vice versa. When it comes to new action, there is nothing more powerful than specificity without imposition, because specificity means clarity and without imposition means voluntarism. We need new specificity; it needs to be systemwide. It can't be imposed (for one thing, we need to develop more specificity; for another, change never works if imposed). The advantage of our model is that people are attracted to it and fairly quickly start getting to the new specificity. Precision without prescription is powerful.

Underpinning our new paradigm is a radically new purpose for education. We saw above that the old purpose (custodial, sorting, and narrow academics) failed badly, especially in this century. The disruption caused by the pandemic is terrible, but we can look for a few silver linings.

One is that it blew the roof off the present system, exposing problems, but also enabling students, teachers, and parents to "see the system," so to speak. Second, it has indicated who might be some of our better allies (see Fullan, 2022). Yes, many have become exhausted, depressed, and less hopeful. But many are also more open than ever to alternatives. Our drivers framework was built on these conditions: first, from 2014 to 2019 when people simply found less and less purpose in regular schooling, and then in 2020 to 2023 when people became desperate (or open to more radical alternatives). Humans yearn for purpose and thrive when it becomes possible. That possibility is now before us for the next few years!

Humans yearn for purpose and thrive
when it becomes possible. That possibility is now
before us for the next few years!

We have captured this moment in the humanity paradigm which has been brewing for the past decade (2014 onward) and has become crystallized by experiences in the pandemic. The humanity paradigm consists of actions taken to enable all living things to cope, develop, and flourish under the complicated and adverse conditions of complex societies. This paradigm is poised to accelerate and expand under the right conditions. Our purpose in this book is to provide substance, definition, and momentum at this fork in the road for humanity.

We start by defining briefly the four drivers, including a chart (Figure 1.1) that identifies the main specific elements within each driver.

DEFINING THE FOUR DRIVERS

FIGURE 1.1 ● The Humanity Paradigm

The humanity paradigm consists of actions taken to enable all living things to cope, develop, and flourish under the complicated and adverse conditions of complex society.

A "driver" is a force that attracts power and generates motion and energy on a continuous basis in a desirable direction.

A "driver" is a force that attracts power and generates motion and energy on a continuous basis in a desirable direction.

- **Driver 1: Well-Being and Learning**—*recognizes that people can no longer survive unless they have a sense of purpose, belonging, and safety in society combined with dynamic learning.*

- **Driver 2: Social and Machine Intelligence**—*consists of individual and group capacities to critically appraise and use technology, including artificial intelligence (AI) for the benefit of humankind and the universe.*

- **Driver 3: Equity-Equality Investments**—*denotes the development of resources to support equity (fairness of initial investment in developing people and society) that produce greater equality (outcomes that reduce the gap among individuals and groups of people) and increase prosperity for all.*

- **Driver 4: Systemness**—*when people become aware that they are part of a larger entity, and strive to understand their own context, as they build connections with other levels in order to improve the system as a whole. Rebuilding the system by building the base (local), mobilizing the middle (region), and intriguing the top.*

In subsequent chapters we develop the detailed meaning of each driver along with concrete examples of the driver in action. The key elements within the drivers are captured in Figure 1.2.

FIGURE 1.2 ● Elements of Each Driver

1. Well-Being and Learning	• Feeling safe and valued • Having purpose and meaning • Regulating stress • Having caring relationships • Developing Learning Competencies for solving complex problems
2. Social and Machine Learning	• Being proactive with technology in relation to Well-Being and Learning • Appraising technology with respect to Equity-Equality biases • Increasing individual and group capacities to use technology to maximize Well-Being and Learning for all
3. Equity-Equality Investments	• Supporting macro Equity-Equality strategies, such as tax reform, poverty reduction, job creation, fair wages, mental and physical health, community development, career paths, early childhood, and the like • Engaging in local Equity-Equality practices: community schools, family health centers, homelessness, food, shelter, and safety
4. Systemness	• Enlarging your local sense of identity within your school and community and across schools in the district (networks) • Considering how schools/community and the district can achieve greater coherence and collective identity • Fostering a "we-we" identity within your school district/network • Considering how you can engage the base, mobilize the middle, and intrigue the top • Rebuilding the system from the ground up with crisscrossing action within and across the levels

Together, our sets of drivers operate as a new system development enterprise within which there are four crucial dynamics.

1. First, the drivers feed on each other; they are a system, and you have to use them as such—always thinking through their inter-dynamics.

2. Second, they have to be usable by the average practitioner—say, the average ten-year-old—comprehensible by the regular participant.

3. Third, we recognize that the third and fourth drivers seem like a tall order. Are we serious that regular people, including young ones, can make a direct contribution to *changing the system in relation to policy investments and Systemness?* Actually, yes. Experts are not able to make much headway on their own, but common learning on scale may be able to generate breakthroughs.

4. Fourth, the drivers in concert form a dynamic synergy to rock and change existing systems for the betterment of humankind and the system.

Existing systems do not welcome change. In *Glass Onion: A Knives Out Mystery,* director Rian Johnson's (2022) quirky satire on the absurdity of the mega-wealthy, one of the characters says, "As it turns out, no one wants you to break the system itself." We say those inside the (ineffective) system, particularly at the bottom and middle, may be the best bets for breaking (transforming) the system. *Drivers are about breaking the status quo by transforming it.*

COHERENCE MAKING

Coherence making, as we said, is "the shared sense of understanding of the nature of the work." The work of the drivers is complex—the development of shared understanding of the drivers individually, and in combination, will be no mean feat. Prior to the pandemic, well-being had taken a back seat to learning. Sometimes ill-being was missed altogether because of racism and other forms of bigotry. If it was considered, it was seen as a barrier to learning. Advances in neuroscience changed that paradigm as educators and others began to see the upward power of well-being, not only to help students survive but also to thrive, surpassing the boundaries of what was thought to be possible for all. During the pandemic, people became so sensitized to ill-being that if a student failed to come to school a teacher would more likely worry about their physical and mental health than how much learning they might be missing. And probably for the first time, many teachers found that their students had much more upward potential than they had realized. Neuroscience amplified learning in other ways. We and others found that relationships and pedagogy grounded in the culture of students magnify Well-Being and Learning, especially the way they feed on each other (see also, for example, Duncan-Andrade, 2022): two aspects, bound together as one synthetic driver. You will see examples of how this works in our vignettes. Ill-being can be addressed while well-being for all becomes the goal. Becoming good at learning and good at life for all becomes the universal goal.

In other words, self-actualization for individuals is not the end goal. In the early 1940s, American psychologist Abraham Maslow identified a series of human needs that ranged from physiological and safety needs to self-actualization. There is some doubt whether Maslow intended it as a hierarchy and whether self-actualization was the endpoint. In any case, public education has lost its way by allowing individual accomplishment to become the end-all-and-be-all. We will show that the *combination* of individual development, group and community betterment, and world preservation and enhancement is the essence of education and learning for the future. Individual fulfillment in the context of collective development that benefits the universe is the driver.

Earlier in this chapter we reported on Goldin and Katz's (2008) study of the race between technology and education. Driver 2 speaks to a more fascinating race: the race between human and machine intelligence. AI first appeared in fiction more than 100 years ago, then in science about seventy-five years ago. AI took off while we were sleeping, in much the same period that economic inequality flourished beneath the surface in the 1980s to the present period. There is an evolutionary pattern here. Maybe humans like to be caught napping and then rise to the occasion. We will examine some great analyses of AI in Chapter 3. The question is: Does human development have to take a back seat to AI? Our response is an emphatic no! The driver is social intelligence at work.

An interesting phenomenon took place, literally while we were writing this book. It seemed pretty clear in 2022, for example, that humans were wary of technology (and we shall argue in Chapter 3 that we still should be). But virtually all of a sudden, in November 2022 to be precise, something happened. A group called Open AI announced and released ChatGPT—a family of large language models that could generate in a matter of seconds a polished essay on any topic imaginable. And it did just that, made free to the public. At roughly the same time, law professor Orly Lobel (2022) published her book *The Equality Machine* with the subtitle *Harnessing Digital Technology for a Brighter More Inclusive Future*. The case was made that perhaps the best driver might be social intelligence figuring out how to team up with machine intelligence! Nobody has said paradigm shifts would be easy, but we now have a problem worth grappling with. The driver is Social and Machine Intelligence in combination.

Equity and *equality*—terms that are often used interchangeably—have different meanings and impacts. Merriam-Webster differentiates the terms this way: *Equality* means the state of being equal, and *equity* adds the element of justice or fairness; it's possible that equal treatment does not produce equity when conditions and circumstances are very different. Equity is about fairness, especially at the start of a given change process, and equality is about better *outcomes* that reduce inequality. *Equity-equality investments* denote the need for resources to achieve greater equity of opportunity, resulting in greater equality of outcomes.

Equality *means the state of being equal, and equity adds the element of justice or fairness; it's possible that equal treatment does not produce equity when conditions and circumstances are very different.*

Investments in equity, intended to bring about more equal outcomes, for example, have been enormous in the past seventy-five years, but to little avail. This outcome is partly because we have siloed equity investments—failing to make them part of the integrated fabric of system reform. Equity investments must become integrated with overall system development. The war on poverty and education for all is intimately interrelated. Unequal societies harm everyone (Wilkinson & Pickett, 2019). Ultimately, the system of accountability must become a *system of comprehensive development*: health, food, shelter, safety, early learning, community, health and education workers. Such work is now underway. With this driver, we want to see the relationship between equity investments (such as reducing poverty) and improved equality outcomes (such as less poverty and more life success).

Longtime systems guru Peter Senge and his colleague Mette Böll (2023) at the Massachusetts Institute of Technology have developed a Compassion Systems Awareness Certificate for practitioners. It is a great program that supplies individuals trained in system leadership. For system change on scale, we will need vastly more people than Senge and his team. Later in our vignettes we will introduce the 6Cs: character/compassion, citizenship, collaboration, communication, creativity, and critical thinking. In combination, the 6Cs make a significant contribution to better Systemness. In effect, the new education must supply graduates who have increased their system acumen as part of normal universal learning. This is not as impractical as it sounds. Young people have a natural propensity for such learning. In the new paradigm, system work is done as an integral part of learning from day one and all the way through. In related work on leadership, we have named "becoming a system player" as a key attribute of effective leaders, such as principals (Fullan, 2023a).

In system terms, we will make the case that we need to build the base (students, teachers, and their local communities), mobilize the middle (districts and regions), and intrigue the top (policy level). The latter is a bit of a playful entry into a complex phenomenon. Essentially, we need to redefine the role of the top (policy level). They need to invest in developments of the other two levels, learn from successes and failures, and refine accountability to focus on progress and what can be learned from it. In extreme cases they need to intervene, but mostly they must be intrigued to learn what makes for success, and then establish strategies to leverage greater success on a wider basis. In Chapter 5 on Systemness we will spell out what we mean by tri-level interactive Systemness in action.

To meet Kuhn's (1962) definition of a "radically different and better paradigm" depends on transforming learning from its current state to one that affects all students very differently than does the present system. The new purpose should be to help young people cope with an increasingly complex world, including competencies to do well under circumstances never before experienced. We see well-being associated with thriving—intertwined in what we call Deep Learning: the ability to learn how to learn, know oneself, and know about "the other" and the environment. Deep Learning (Chapter 6) is an integrated approach that supports the drivers in accomplishing the system transformation that we badly need.

The new purpose should be to help young people cope with an increasingly complex world, including competencies to do well under circumstances never before experienced.

We are also discovering a new role for *leadership*. First, we find many of the best ideas are generated in our interactions with practitioners. The more difficult the situation, and the closer you are to it, the more the learning *if* the four drivers are your guide. Second, we need leadership that can mobilize and jointly determine the best direction by acting together, including sorting out what works best. Note closely the role of leaders in the vignettes in each chapter. Fullan (2023a) just released a book called *The Principal 2.0*, which contains eight case studies of school principals where the overall conclusion is that the main role of the principal should be to develop the *internal system* at the local school and community level linking laterally and upward as they carry out their roles. Look for more examples of local leadership from "students as changemakers," and leadership within communities develops. In all cases, there needs to be the generation of ideas and action locally, coordinating leadership at all levels, and degrees of freedom at the lower levels combined with *internal accountability*. The latter includes our nuanced but powerful new concept—*specificity without imposition*—which combines seeking specific solutions at the source of action with a degree of voluntarism, and sharing of what is being learned and accomplished. Leadership is dispersed but coordinated. It is crucial that the system cultivates transformation through different relationships within and across the three levels of local, middle, and center.

There is one more intriguing perspective to take on schools and social change. We are supportive of other movements that support social change *outside of public schools*. But we raise the question that maybe these external to school initiatives represent end runs to an unresponsive public school system. For most societal priorities, external forays will not be sufficient. For example, the fight about climate change has been going on since the 1960s. More progress was made in terms of public pressure in the past century than in the current one. Our interpretation of Naomi Klein and Rebecca Stefoff's (2021) *How to Change Everything: The Young Human's Guide to Protecting the Planet and Each Other*, is that the greatest public presence about the dangers of climate change was from 1967 to 1989, followed by a clawback period by big business, oil companies, and others from 1990 to 2017 (Klein & Stefoff, 2021).

In 2018, at the age of fifteen, Greta Thunberg took off school (ironically) and stepped into the bigger picture. Allow us an interesting hypothesis. Notice that the decline of action on climate that Klein and Stefoff (2021) depict started in the first phase—say around 1975. This decline coincided almost exactly with when education began its stall. We don't for a moment think that this is a causal relationship. But we do think that Thunberg *plus* schools and their students working together could have made a difference. In the absence of good education for all, ad hoc political action has little chance for success. Social movements, such as in the golden age above (1967 to 1989), have little chance of success if not accompanied by congruent changes in public education. We need systems working on system change!

When Fullan was an early teenager in the 1950s growing up in the east end of Toronto, there was a famous American bank robber named Willie Sutton (1901–1980) coming to the end of his forty-year career. He was purportedly asked by a reporter, "Why do you rob banks?" His response was, "Because that's where the money is."

If you want to reduce climate change, help the disadvantaged, and create a more equal society, transform schools *because that's where the kids are!*

If you want to reduce climate change, help the disadvantaged, and create a more equal society, transform schools because that's where the kids are!

Driver 1:
Well-Being and Learning

1

Recognizes that people can no longer survive unless they have a sense of purpose and belonging in society combined with dynamic learning.

4 SYSTEMNESS

Coherence Making

3 EQUITY-EQUALITY INVESTMENTS

2 SOCIAL AND MACHINE INTELLIGENCE

Elements

- Feeling safe and valued

- Having purpose and meaning

- Regulating stress

- Having caring relationships

- Developing Learning Competencies for solving complex problems

. . . .

CHAPTER 2

Driver 1
Well-Being and Learning

I n each of the next four chapters, we will examine a case vignette that illustrates the driver in action. These vignettes will not capture the driver in full but will provide an illustration of how various education systems use the basic strategies and concepts to improve their systems, especially enhancing the lives of students, teachers, other educators, parents, and communities. Well-being, as we noted in Chapter 1, is about purpose, meaning, belonging, and working individually and with others to solve problems and make a contribution in a complex and dangerous universe. It is simultaneously about coping with adversity and learning to create better futures.

THE DOUBLE HELIX OF HUMAN THRIVING

In complex societies, well-being is not secure unless it is combined with dynamic learning. Well-being and learning feed on each other. They are, if you like, *the double helix of human thriving* (Figure 2.1).

In complex societies, well-being is not secure unless it is combined with dynamic learning. Well-being and learning feed on each other.

FIGURE 2.1 ● The Double Helix of Human Thriving

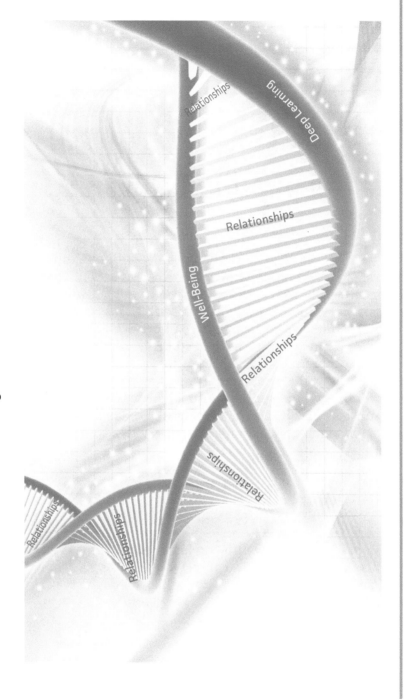

It is crucial that we understand the combination of Well-Being and Learning and their relationship to coping and developing in a challenging world, especially if students come from conditions of poverty and other disadvantages. Well-being is not just energy and happiness. It also the struggles and breakthroughs. Driver 3—Equity-Equality Investments—includes success under extremely difficult circumstances. We think the drivers and related Deep Learning (Chapter 6) provide the opportunity for struggling students to succeed, as they enable all students to become changemakers in a society that desperately needs citizens who can be effective individually and in groups.

As we noted in Chapter 1, the threefold purpose of individual, community, and societal development is a new and expanded purpose for schooling that is essential for our future and our relation to the planet and the universe. The development and synergy of the four drivers represent how we will survive and thrive in a future that has boundless upward potential but is also vulnerable to catastrophe.

The threefold purpose of individual, community, and societal development is a new and expanded purpose for schooling that is essential for our future and our relation to the planet and the universe.

Over the years, well-being has often been referred to as an educational goal, but it never stuck (as compared to academic goals, such as literacy, numeracy, and science). Suddenly it seemed to jump onto center stage as a result of the combination of two big structural problems, along with the pandemic. The two big structural issues—climate collapse and gross inequality—had been brewing for more than a century. Climate deterioration has become increasingly comprehensive in its dimensions, deadly on every front (Wallace-Wells, 2019). It is not as if there were no warnings. How much clearer can you get than the 2012 United Nations Intergovernmental Panel on Climate Change: "A changing climate leads to changes in the frequency, intensity, duration, and timing of extreme weather and climate events." The other structural failure concerns mounting health and social problems. People in Western societies are no longer increasing life expectancy; quality of life, on average, is worsening. Social trust (the degree to which people trust other groups in society) has plunged in the past sixty-five years (Putnam & Garrett, 2020).

COVID-19 really brought home the direct connection between our planet and the human condition. Virtually everyone knows close relatives and friends who have died. Stories of extreme deprivation are reported in the news every day. Examples of mounting anxiety, mental illness, and extreme stress became commonplace. For the first time, mental health has become everyone's problem. Stress, anxiety, and loss became emotionally vivid in almost everyone's life. In addition, these stresses became linked to loss of learning, missed school, and academic performance. People experienced ill-being as a direct link to the deterioration of life.

The silver lining was the realization that well-being is not only a cure for ill-being; when combined with dynamic learning it is also the gateway to a much better life than we might have settled for. The realization emerged that traditional academic-based schooling might be placing unnecessary limits on what we could learn, not just placing limited expectations on certain groups, but underestimating what humans more generally could accomplish.

The silver lining was the realization that well-being is not only a cure for ill-being; when combined with dynamic learning is also the gateway to a much better life than we might have settled for.

An almost shocking possibility came to the fore, namely that the strong stress on academic learning by itself may be bad for your mental health! Put positively, there may be more to success in life than academic grades (or, if you prefer, a different approach may increase and deepen academic learning for all, including grades, while adding competencies more suited to flourishing in complex systems). All of this put a new spotlight on schooling. The experience of the pandemic and its associated ramifications in a deep way has given us a wake-up call. We began to question seriously: What is the meaning of our existence? And why are we on this planet anyway?

We have already made the point that academic learning has become less and less relevant, as *an end in itself* for more and more students. When we factor in racism and other inequities it gets worse. In his brilliant in-depth examination, *Equality or Equity*, Jeffrey Duncan-Andrade (2022) states:

> For young people whose lives are replete with social stressors over which they feel little control (racism, poverty, violence, patriarchy . . . lack of access to nutrition, substandard education, substandard health care), their systems are forced to work overtime all the time. (p. 34)

Getting closer to our main point, Duncan-Andrade says we have taught kids the mechanical skills of reading, writing, and arithmetic "without the explicit intention of using them to deepen our wellness" (p. 154). He further concludes that "as long we keep talking about academic rigor and social justice as if they are somehow separate, we are doing neither. There is no rigor without relationships, relevance, and our responsibility to social justice. And there is no social justice without rigor" (p. 185). Put another way, we have siloed equity, and that is why it has failed.

In short, *academic obsession is not a primary motivator, but wellness linked to learning is an intrinsic and powerful stimulus for individual and collective action!* We learned the hard way about relentless stress and ill-being. The link to climate collapse and gross inequality prompted other major reasons to change. Add to that the stress of boredom and alienation in schooling and we have mounting pressure to do something. Once we add "new learning" to the equation we have the makings of a solution.

STUDENTS AS CHANGEMAKERS

We find this breakthrough in the inclination of children and youth. Many are mired and destroyed by extreme prejudice and crippling poverty, but the potential for liberation, and the reasons for so doing at this state of human evolution, are powerful. Fullan's (2022) op-ed "6 Reasons Why We Should See Students as Changemakers" further makes the case:

SIX REASONS OUR STUDENTS SHOULD BE SEEN AS CHANGEMAKERS

1. Young people have the most at stake.

2. Kids have an evolutionary instinct to take action.

3. The best directional solutions are becoming known.

4. Too many children are now "lost."

5. We could be making better investments.

6. Discovering and developing unimaginable better futures makes life worth living.

Source: Fullan (2022).

As young people progress through Deep Learning we expect and enable them to develop the Global Competencies–6Cs (character/compassion, citizenship, collaboration, communication, creativity, and critical thinking) while developing their Well-Being and Learning. All this happens while working in partnership with others inside and outside the school. Well-being and new learning is the foundational driver for overall development. It is centered around the three fundamental goals of education: individual development and contribution, community development, and societal betterment. Academic learning occurs within this combination because it is required for success in all three dimensions— individual, group, and society. It is essential that academic learning occurs naturally in the course of pursuing Well-Being and Learning. The latter must be made prominent because old habits of academic learning can neglect well-being, and even inhibit Deep Learning. Well-being and learning together is a human integrator in the pursuit of deeper individual and collective goals that benefit both human and nonhuman life. What is also noteworthy is that it was the perils of COVID that brought ill-being/well-being into the spotlight. In effect, the pandemic brought Well-Being and Learning to the fore. Sometimes humans need a powerful external catalyst to enable breakthrough.

We selected one of our founding members in our Deep Learning network, the Ottawa Catholic School Board (OCSB), as our first exemplar with respect to Well-Being and Learning. As you read the vignette, consider these action guidelines for reflection and discussion with colleagues.

ACTION GUIDELINES FOR WELL-BEING AND LEARNING

- Rate the overall energy level in your school/community (on a scale from 1 to 10).

  List the main stressors.

  List the main positive things your community benefits from.

- Discuss with your leadership team: What are your highest hopes, and what are your worst fears, for the immediate future of your community?

- With your leadership team: Give a brief overview of the four drivers. What key features stand out the most?

- Reread Chapter 2 and discuss with your team how you might get started on Driver 1.

Driver 1 Vignette

Ottawa Catholic School Board

Ottawa Catholic School Board (OCSB) is one of seventy-two publicly funded school districts in Ontario, Canada. In 2014, OCSB was one of the founding members of New Pedagogies for Deep Learning (NPDL) (https://deep-learning.global). At the time, the director (superintendent) was Denise Andre; Tom D'Amico, who was associate director, is now the director. OCSB consists of 47,000 students in eighty-three schools. The district continues to grow and is currently building an additional four elementary schools.

The schools in OCSB are located across urban, suburban, and rural areas. In Ottawa, the population is identified as Indigenous (2.5%) and visible minorities (25%). Black, Chinese, and Arab make up the largest groups of visible minorities in Ottawa (Statistics Canada, 2021).

Based on academic measures—literacy, numeracy, high school graduation—it has been one of the top-performing school districts of the seventy-two in the province. OCSB joined because it was seeking new ideas and access to learning from other schools in Canada and worldwide. It was also attracted to learning about the 6Cs—character/compassion, citizenship, collaboration, communication, creativity, and critical thinking—and implementing them as foundational for the district.

We had worked with the district before and knew that it valued innovation and pursued it in close consultation with its schools (what we call joint determination). It also had a Systemness perspective—the idea of having all schools working together in what we now refer to as connected autonomy. Through consultation it joined NPDL with seven schools—representing each of the seven geographical regions within the district. Twelve months later they added another eight schools, and at the end of two years expanded to all eighty-three schools adopting Deep Learning. The district used the opportunity to promote new learning (linking pedagogy to learning goals) while establishing a baseline of technology to support it.

By 2018 we had published our basic book on Deep Learning, titled *Deep Learning: Engage the World Change the World* (Fullan et al., 2018). The whole Deep Learning initiative and model had evolved through collaboration, central coordination, and mutual influence between and among member networks. It is perhaps no coincidence (given how proactive they are) that by 2018 OCSB adopted a new board strategic plan, which underscored three new board commitments: "Be Community," "Be Well," and "Be Innovative." Note that this was prior to COVID. This is not a small point. At a time when COVID-19 did not exist in the minds of educators and the public, OCSB *intuited* that well-being and community were foundational goals. It was also during this time that Associate Director Tom D'Amico became director as Denise Andre retired—a smooth transition if there ever was one.

While COVID gained strength in 2020, OCSB was out of the gate immediately with a series of emotional support actions both small and large scale that embraced everyone in the district. It was clear that these were not just stop-gap actions. Some involved emergency actions, while others built in new cutting-edge innovations (such as a major initiative on social entrepreneurship led by students). Well-being sensitivity and actions came to the fore not as ad hoc, but as opportunities to integrate Well-Being and Learning.

When D'Amico was interviewed about how school leadership fared during the pandemic he said:

> Relationship building continues to be a key priority for administrators to meet with success. The Board's strategic commitments are "Be Community," "Be Innovative," and "Be Well." All administrators provide oversight of the Board's implementation of the Deep Learning framework in their school.
>
> The interconnectedness of the school to its local community and the global political realities is a new challenge and opportunity for school principals. Principals in today's schools must understand the realities of past miscarriages of justice, such as the impact of residential schools on multi-generations of Indigenous Peoples. There are new opportunities for Indigenous ways of teaching and learning partnerships with community elders, along with school improvement plans that include a focus on truth and reconciliation.
>
> Today's principal needs to understand their privileged position and the power that comes with the role. Principals need to learn and grow in all areas of equity work with their staff and students. Providing true voice to students and staff from traditionally marginalized communities needs to be part of today's principal skill set. There are many opportunities to move from tokenism to authentic agency when the principal focuses on listening and creates school and community learning partnerships. Today's principal needs to use their network to create expanded learning partnerships between classes, across grades, across schools, and across district boundaries and borders.

Principals have always been lifelong learners; however, today's principal needs to spend time self-reflecting to have a better understanding of the biases that they may bring with them into their role. In the OCSB all aspiring leaders must demonstrate an understanding of how Deep Learning is a needed reform in education. All administrators in the OCSB taking part in interview teams must have first completed an antibias interviewing course.

A previous cohort of principals needed to recognize the importance of using technology and moving from substitution to redefinition for transformation—the SAMR model (Substitution Augmentation Modification Redefinition). Today's principals need to focus on how technology can be used to level the playing field for those traditionally marginalized and to provide equity of access to all in their school community. Most importantly, today's principal needs to focus on the humane use of technology.

As the school community, staff, and students become more diverse, the role of the principal continues to evolve. School principals need to be creative to ensure that their school and curriculum are representative of those that both serve. A focus on learning partnerships and building community is one way for school principals to grow in this area. Principals must continue to focus on pedagogical practices and must "use the group to move the group." What has changed for today's principal is that the key leaders to move the group may come from the staff, from students, or from the community.

The complexities of the school and competing community demands, also dictate that principals need to build their conflict resolution skills. Dealing with conflict needs to focus on both student conflict and adult conflict in today's school environment.

As schools transform into learning environments that focus on both academic achievement and staff and student well-being, the role of the principal must also change. The traditional view of the principal as the charismatic leader that can do it all must change. The

OCSB has adopted a view that promotes distributed leadership and uses the talents amongst all the staff, the students, and the community, as the leadership model that is positioned to deal with the complexities of today's school environment.

The role of the principal is no longer to prepare students for the future, but rather to help staff and students make a difference in their world today, in order to build a better future together. (D'Amico, personal interview, 2022)

When D'Amico was asked to name a principal who would be representative of the view of school leaders in the district, he suggested JP Cloutier, who has been a secondary educator with the district for more than twenty years (JP Cloutier also appears as a case vignette in *The Principal 2.0*, Fullan, 2023a). Cloutier understands the important skill of administrators forming meaningful relationships with students and supporting learning environments that extend beyond the confines of a classroom.

The role of the principal now requires astute political awareness and an understanding of the global context that the school is part of. After building his network of colleagues at two different high schools as vice principal, Cloutier was promoted to the role of principal in 2020. Notre Dame is a Grade 7–12 school of about 700 students. The school is designated as a children's support school by the board and is part of the Ontario Ministry of Education Urban Priority high school initiative. This initiative provides support for students to improve literacy and numeracy skills while connecting with their community and learning valuable leadership skills that might not otherwise be available to them. Through a partnership with Dovercourt Recreation Centre, the school offers free programming at the end of the school day from 3:00 to 5:30 p.m. Every day, students can sign up for any number of student services: tutoring, swimming, music, drama, leadership, and so on.

Cloutier's focus on learning partnerships has helped Notre Dame connect students to their individual passions both inside and outside of the classroom. The school has partnered with technology company Ciena to participate in the Ciena solutions challenge sponsored by Digital Promise. Using relationship-building strategies, students become partners in the learning environment. Students have opportunities to select their own learning activities and have a voice in their learning. Leveraging technology to make a difference in the lives of others has helped to turn students into creators where they could impact their school and the local community. The pride and excitement of student learning are highlighted by Cloutier when he intentionally celebrates innovative teachers on his staff. The Ciena solutions challenge is a practical example of Deep Learning in action as students express pride in their learning and how they use technology to make a difference.

In response to the Black Lives Matter movement, students at Notre Dame wanted to make a difference. The students from the Black Student Association (BSA) worked outside of class to come up with the design for a Black Lives Matter school T-shirt and sweatshirt. Cloutier was aware of the passion that these students had for what was happening around the world and recognized his ability to provide them with a platform for their voice. In his privileged position as principal, he worked with the students to modify the school uniform policy and allow the Black Lives Matter shirts to be worn as part of the school uniform. The funds generated from the sale of shirts were donated to the Agnes Zabali Boys and Girls Club in Uganda, a club created by a former Notre Dame high school graduate, Jimmy Sebulime. Cloutier created opportunities for the students to share their experience with the media, at a board meeting, and with other schools across the city. This learning activity and experience happened outside of the class and has given students true agency in making a difference in their local school, across their community, and across borders. The students from the BSA shared their experience with other school BSAs and then with the director of education as part of the Black Student Advisory Council. This resulted in boardwide changes to the school uniform and dress code policies. This is learning that sticks, and the students will never forget the impact they had.

When asked to reflect on the definition of the modern principal in 2022, Cloutier responded:

> Principals are professional collaborators. In my view, the main role of the principal today is to lead change by implementing the board's vision while responding to the specific needs of the school community. To drive change, we build community and capacity by leading from the middle.
>
> We have a responsibility to both follow and lead as we collaborate with system leaders and consultants who provide guidance and hear our concerns; principals from other schools as we share ideas and resources; staff members who learn alongside us and share their views; families and community partners; and, most importantly, the students who we serve. These relationships are central to the principal's role as community builder.
>
> We care about our school communities and position ourselves as learners. As we build relationships and look for opportunities for staff and students, we develop a greater understanding of how we can contribute to both the school and the system at large. With this understanding, we are able to respond to the needs of our communities and leverage our position to support student learning.
>
> Looking forward, a widespread desire among educators for a better normal makes this a very exciting time to be a principal. While the OCSB strategic commitments and the Deep Learning framework have been a focus for many years, the challenges presented in recent years have highlighted their necessity if we want our students to seize the future, however uncertain it might be.
>
> Equity drives our actions in education, and principals must continue to be allies for staff, students, and school communities. Principals are in a position to support staff members both in their learning and in their efforts to provide students the means to achieve. Most importantly, in the pursuit of equitable outcomes for each student in our system, principals must continue to take a learning role.

I am inspired by both the students demonstrating global citizenship right now and the innovative educators providing them with the opportunities to do so. The students and staff working together towards change are setting a strong example for what is possible. There is much to be gained by taking this moment to make a difference rather than waiting for tomorrow. (Cloutier, personal interview, 2022)

Well-being and learning are, almost by definition, expansive concepts. They are something that is perhaps grown initially at home but is spontaneously extended, well, to the world at large. As we head toward a new future, one that we consider in this book to present a unique opportunity to create a new model, D'Amico's first instinct is to reach outside to create an opportunity to consider the future in light of the difficulties and opportunities that may be before us.

In contemplating the return to school in September 2022—the first full year since the pandemic began in March 2020—D'Amico did not say "Let's regroup, let's just support each other." Instead, with the full support of the board and staff, he announced in August a public event for October 3–4 to which he invited all Canadian schools and districts that were involved in Deep Learning. I asked him why he was putting on such a labor-intensive event when people were returning after a very difficult two years. In his response, he clearly saw the occasion as an energizer or perhaps more naturally because that is who we are and what we do. In his words:

In August, prior to the start of the school, we did run a conference for our staff. We had sixty-seven breakout sessions offered by fifty-seven different staff. Close to 900 educators took part. As part of the application process to present, each presenter had to indicate which of the four elements of Deep Learning their presentation connected to. The topics cover everything from equity, math, de-streaming, kindergarten, new teachers, outdoor education, teaching religion, social-emotional learning, etc. It's a good way to use Deep Learning to frame our work, without having a conference that is specific to Deep Learning. (D'Amico, personal interview, 2022)

With respect to the October 3–4, 2022, event, D'Amico described its purpose as:

> Prior to the pandemic we always welcomed visitors from other countries and districts into our schools for visits. This is a great opportunity for our staff and students to learn about other countries or districts and build learning partnerships. The visits are a great way of affirming the good work happening in schools, and it also serves as a push-pull driver for Deep Learning in the district. When a principal knows that visitors will be coming to their school, they usually have a focused discussion with their family of school superintendent, and it gives them another opportunity to be in their classes and use the language of Deep Learning with their staff. Targeted visits to schools help the admin team take a learning stance regarding the work that still needs to be done in their school to build capacity and ensure that all students have opportunities for rich learning experiences, not just those that are with the most talented educators.
>
> Our senior team tracks all Board visits during the year and we try to ensure that a wide range of schools are selected (i.e., inner-city schools, new schools, old schools), and this helps our team focus on system change, and not just on a few high-achieving schools. (D'Amico, personal interview, 2022)

An interesting exchange happened on October 4 when a group of visitors (including Fullan) were at Notre Dame high school, where Cloutier is principal. A group of educators from other provinces across Canada had just finished touring the school and were talking informally with some students. One student (Grade 11) was being asked questions about what the school was like. After responding generally that it was a great school, one of the educators pressed the student with the question, "What is it like for you, personally, as a student?" The student instantly responded with a three-minute animated soliloquy that started with how he had hated school in Grade 7 (dragged himself to school, slept at his desk, etc.), and now he can't wait to get to school—everyone supports him, it's a large secondary school, he is learning a great deal, people care about each other, it's like a big family, etc.

One of our team members was watching and listening to this exchange, which was being filmed on a cell phone. She went over to Cloutier who was standing on the other side of the room and said to him, "You should get a copy of that video and show it on school program nights and events as a promotion of the school." He instantly responded, "No, I am going to show it to his mother!"

We call this "contextually literate."

Before we leave Ottawa, let us consider one other matter—a crucial question concerning the future of learning. The big question is: If standardized tests focusing on academic goals are not the best outcome measure, what is the alternative? Conscious of this issue, in September 2019 OCSB launched a systemwide focus on the Global Competencies. The goal was that every staff member and every student could state the competency or competencies (among the 6Cs) that they would identify in the school improvement plan as a focus. The district indicated that in order for students to self-assess the selected competency, they needed to understand what the competency means for them and how they could demonstrate and improve in this competency. The goal was skill development in the selected competency and not for a formal mark. As D'Amico put it, "Ideally for true learning we want intrinsic motivation, not extrinsic motivation, to improve the competency from the beginning of the year to the end" (D'Amico, personal communication, 2022).

In October and November 2019, the district held systemwide staff meetings to work on the assessment of the Global Competencies, including further preparation for student self-reporting on progress with respect to given competencies. Of this, D'Amico explained, "We had staff look at how to incorporate Global Competencies within the learning skills on the report card" (D'Amico, personal communication, 2022). Along came COVID in early March 2020, which caused the competency assessment plan to be deferred, with an interest to revisit the development. If there is any consolation, there is now a greater worldwide interest in revamping the student assessment question. We will return to this key matter later in the book.

All in all, OCSB's behavior, whether it is inside or external, always focuses on Well-Being and Learning, which they extend beyond their borders. That is why we consider it as part and parcel of Driver 1. We want these vignettes to feature one driver at a time so that we can get deeper into each concept. However, we would not have selected the case if it did not have evidence of all four drivers in action. Each driver draws you to the others. It is the interaction effect that gets the results. As OCSB pursued Well-Being and Learning they also focused on collaboration, use of technology, equality investments so that all schools flourished, and they exemplified Systemness (we could have selected any number of schools to feature in our visit). OCSB exemplifies proactive Systemness. In 2019, they were systematically developing a new approach to assessing learning outcomes (Global Competencies, not just academic subjects) when the province was not at all considering this matter.

COHERENCE MAKING

If you focus only on Well-Being and Learning, we can't promise transformation. For the latter, you need all four drivers. Driver 1 does represent a foundational start, but it is not the full picture. We can't say this enough: The four drivers depend on each other to get the full force of transformational system change. Instead of a single focus, keep all four drivers in mind as you work with anyone.

We put special stock in the young as changemakers—a role that many of them are desperate to undertake, has enormous possibilities that could be mobilized in a relatively short time frame, and that could have a major impact over the next decade; change that is transformational not just improvement (see Fullan, 2022). We know for a fact that OCSB has been steadily developing students as changemakers in its new work (see https://www.ocsb.ca).

The pandemic has both widened and deepened coherence making in OCSB. New learning has been developed, tried, and assessed with input from all. Students, staff, and community members constantly consider new possibilities, try them out, and debate their efficacy. There are cross-visits with schools to examine the latest innovations. What is working or needs further development is the subject of ongoing conversations. People learn to talk the walk and walk the talk. The flow of information and interaction is such that people get daily practice in coherence making—something that contributes to collective intelligence, individual knowledge, and skill development.

In Ottawa, as well as in all success, Well-Being and Learning become a universal good. We can't think of anything more powerful than to help build the next prototype of the humanity model—and to do so with the young.

We can't think of anything more powerful than to help build the next prototype of the humanity model—and to do so with the young.

Driver 2:
Social and Machine Intelligence

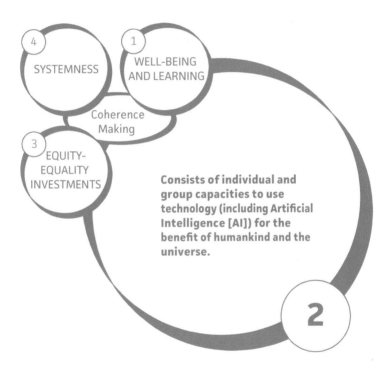

Consists of individual and group capacities to use technology (including Artificial Intelligence [AI]) for the benefit of humankind and the universe.

Elements

- Being proactive with technology in relation to Well-Being and Learning

- Appraising technology with respect to Equity-Equality biases

- Increasing individual and group capacities to use technology to maximize Well-Being and Learning for all

. . . .

CHAPTER 3

Driver 2

Social and Machine Intelligence

We have already referred to Goldin and Katz's (2008) brilliant analysis, *The Race Between Technology and Education.* Here we meet the modern version, "the race between Social and Machine Intelligence," and really, it's like walking into the middle of a movie (it ain't over). We already know that while we were sleeping (1980 to the present) machines (that don't sleep) were racing ahead. The giant intrusion, nay, invasion of ChatGPT in November 2022 will turn out to be the biggest and most needed wake-up call we could ever have received. Rude awakening aside, it serves well Driver 2: mobilizing individual and social intelligence for the betterment of humanity. It makes this driver explicit, and an in-your-face attention getter. Become engaged and proactive because there are no clear a priori predictions that can be made. Become engaged in sorting out what the future of technology may bring as if your life depends on it.

Let's start with the machine side of the story.

MACHINE INTELLIGENCE (ARTIFICIAL INTELLIGENCE)

Meredith Broussard is a data scientist and data journalist at New York University. In 2018, she wrote a book titled *Artificial Unintelligence: How Computers Misunderstand the*

World. She notes that "being good with computers is not the same as being good with people." She makes the point that "computational systems are designed by people who don't care about or don't understand the cultural systems in which we are all embedded" (p. 83). Broussard claims that "when we look at the world through the lens of computation, or we try to solve big social problems using technology alone, we tend to make the same set of predictable mistakes that impeded progress and reinforced inequality" (p. 7).

"Computational systems are designed by people who don't care about or don't understand the cultural systems in which we are all embedded."

Political science professor Virginia Eubanks (2017) confirmed this when she conducted an in-depth study of two automated social services systems (one concerning housing, the other child welfare). Here is her main conclusion:

> What I found was stunning. Across the country, poor and working-class people are targeted by new tools of digital poverty management. . . . Automated eligibility systems discourage them from claiming public resources that they need to survive and thrive. . . . Predictive models and algorithms tag them as risky investments and problematic parents . . . automated decision-making shatters the social safety net, criminalizes the poor, intensifies discrimination, and compromises our deepest human values. (pp. 11–12)

Holmes et al. (2019) of the Center of Curriculum Design in their work, *Artificial Intelligence in Education*, concluded:

> Around the world virtually no research has been undertaken, no guidelines have been provided, no policies have been developed, and no guidelines have been enacted to address the specific ethical issues raised by the use of artificial intelligence in education. (p. 169)

Of course, this review of artificial intelligence (AI) is now outdated with the advent of ChatGPT and its friends. Now we say that with the four drivers, we can turn the tables on AI and determine how we might exploit machine intelligence for the humanity paradigm. We need all four drivers to develop greater social intelligence in order to use machine intelligence for our betterment—an ironic turning of the tables. We still need to develop the human and social capacity to live better than ever with machines.

In the meantime, Meredith Broussard (2023) has just released another book: *More Than a Glitch: Confronting Race, Gender, and Ability Bias in Tech*. Broussard documents case after case in which bias (conscious or not) finds its way into the issues of the day related to race, gender, and ability. Broussard stresses that "Mathematical truth [computers] and social truth [humans] are fundamentally different systems" (p. 2). And that "computers aren't as creative in the way that humans are. They don't have empathy, and they can't come up with alternative solutions or future scenarios as flexibly as humans (at their best) can" (p. 63). Broussard, herself a technologist, makes the case with plenty of examples that technology is more likely to end up (again unwittingly or otherwise) replicating the status quo.

In effect, Broussard argues that our Driver 2—social intelligence—must play a larger role (as we have said, social intelligence has steadily lost the race with technology up to this point) in being able to proactively work with technology. When it comes to our Deep Learning—the humanity paradigm and its goals—there is no way that AI or any combination of machines can do what Anaheim Union High School District (AUHSD) is now developing. Yes, AI might make a system more efficient in what AUHSD calls "the wasteful practice of chasing higher test scores." But AI will never be able to design and carry out the Career Preparedness Systems Framework (CPSF) that is devoted to the well-being and life success of its 28,000 students, and their glorious accomplishments in developing the 5Cs that enable them to become successful students and active citizens to produce a better world (AUHSD essentially focuses on the same Global Competencies as our

6Cs, but have combined our character and citizenship into a single fifth C called character/compassion). AUHSD is a ubiquitous user of technology in the service of preparing students for careers and life (see the AUHSD vignette at the end of this chapter).

Broadly speaking, the status quo has been generated by the same forces that have developed the current technology system—a system that we find so fundamentally wanting. Broussard does not call for the reduction of technology but rather for a more scrutinized and intelligent use. In effect, she calls for a change of drivers with the establishment of a new frame, a Public Interest Technology, defined as: "The application of design, data, and delivery to advance the public interest and promote the public good in the digital age" (from McGuiness & Shank, *Power to the Public*, 2021, as quoted in Broussard, 2023, p. 158).

Not so coincidentally, we find another new book making the same case with much more detail. *The Equality Machine* by San Diego law professor Orly Lobel (2022) advances us down the path of Social and Machine Intelligence and their relationship. Echoing what we already know, Lobel states, "Artificial intelligence (AI), automation, and big data can replicate and exacerbate ongoing injustices" (p. 1). Lobel then lays out a detailed plan for building an equality machine "To embrace digitization as a force for societal good" (p. 5). There are a number of subgoals, such as, "The goal of equality should be embedded in every digital advancement," "We should count what matters," and "We must understand technology as a public good . . . addressing some of the world's toughest problems: global health and pandemics, world hunger, environmental sustainability and climate change, and poverty and inequality" (p. 9) (thereby implicating all four of our drivers).

Lobel's overall stance is, "Technology indeed often embeds inequality. But what if we flipped the script and instead adopted a mindset that inequality faces a tech challenge? What if we considered challenges as opportunities to do better . . . not only to address technology failures, but to use technology to tackle societal failures?" (p. 17). We like her preference "to define fairness in relation to outcomes, not inputs" (p. 31).

More in the realm of our interests, Lobel describes research where robots are contributing to "care work" and the work of educating the next generation (p. 254). Lobel supplies examples showing that "the social integration of robots and the valuing of human care can be mutually reinforcing as society navigates the realities of the future" (p. 265). Perhaps of more interest to us is the work of Cynthia Brezeal at the MIT Media Lab who has developed "social robots" that can relate to children on an emotional level (see her YouTube video, *Developing Social and Empathetic AI,* from 2019, in which personalized robots learn to work with students under the supervision of teachers). Her take on it is that "over time, the robot learns from the interaction with each individual child and personalizes the way it supports the child's learning" (Lobel, 2022, p. 272). And "integrating psychology and the science of learning she designs her robots to mimic peer-to-peer learning" (p. 272). Embodied robots (compared to screen versions) are more effective when children interact with the robot in learning with other children. Breazeal found that "the more the child perceived the robot as social and relational, the more the child showed progress with learning, such as increased vocabulary and verbal growth" (Lobel, 2022, pp. 273–274). Then we have the hypothetical "lost Einsteins" based on research that shows that children's socioeconomic environments are correlated with subsequent learning, i.e., socioeconomic status can limit learning and development for students living in poverty and/or facing bigotry (Bell et al., 2019). How about this for a fantastic hypothesis: Students facing hardship, who have overcome it, make for more effective citizens in a complex world.

Back to technology. We all have been reading about ChatGPT (the AI model released in November 2022 that interacts with humans in a conversational way, seemingly outperforming them on many tasks). By coincidence, as we wrote this paragraph on December 31, 2022, one of our senior team sent a request to ChatGPT: "Write an essay on the validity of equity as an institutional success criterion." Within five seconds, he got a 500-plus-word cogent essay on the topic. The real questions for Driver 2 are: How can we best live in an age of AI? How can we position AI as an asset for humanism? Fortunately, AI is now (May 2023) receiving major attention with arguments on both sides of the coin. Our four drivers in concert offer the best vanguard for an overall systemic solution favoring the humanity paradigm.

Lobel (2022) devotes pages to the dark side of AI, but also to its benefits, such as AI detecting and curing hidden diseases, prosecuting evil networks and prejudices at work, and "challenging cultures of secrecy" (Lobel, p. 102). The bottom line for Lobel is: "Envisioning a path for tomorrow's technology is inextricably tied to exposing the ways that technology harms and creates inequities. But we should be most fearful of being on the outside, merely criticizing without conceiving and creating a brighter future—in researching, designing, prototyping, evaluating and actualizing innovation" (p. 309). Lobel clearly takes a fight-fire-with-fire stance. Equality machines for her are very much social players.

As we write this paragraph, AI looms larger and larger as an unknown force in relation to humanity. On May 1, 2023, a pioneering artificial intelligence researcher named Geoffrey Hinton announced that he quit his position at Google "in order to speak freely about the dangers posed by AI" (Castaldo, 2023). Hinton, also an emeritus professor of computer science at the University of Toronto, worried that AI impaired people's ability to differentiate truth from fiction and could encroach on job losses, including automating away jobs that embody our best humanity. In another article, Wendy Wong, professor of political science at the University of British Columbia, writes, "There are some complex political concepts such as fairness, justice, and ethics that we should recognize do not have definitive answers" (Wong, 2023).

In short, we need to strengthen *social intelligence*, including "values embedded in human rights: autonomy, dignity, equality and community" (Wong, 2023). All of this is a *cri de coeur* from the founders of AI that in effect says, STOP. We must consider our core humanity. Loud and clear it says: Let's make the *drivers*, above all, be the humanity paradigm! Focus on the development of social intelligence, which has seriously lagged technology over the past sixty years.

SOCIAL INTELLIGENCE

We consider individual and social intelligence as a single phenomenon because they so clearly feed on each other. Our preferred concept is 'connected autonomy' (Fullan et al., 2022). People need to be their own person, but they also need to be part of a functioning group (see Driver 1). More than this, we hold the view that humans collectively, for the past fifty or more years, have lagged behind technological advances. Ironically, they have failed the humanity paradigm. Our way forward is very much tied into this supposition that humans, once again, have been asleep at the switch. And that this is the very time to "switch the switch"; moreover, the new paradigm (the drivers) could produce deep change in short order—decades not centuries. And it is backed by the latest research on the neuroscience of learning and well-being (Cantor & Osher, 2021).

In a complex world, individual and social intelligence is at a premium. We need a plan and a corresponding set of actions. Rosemary Luckin (2018) writes in *Machine Learning and Human Intelligence*, "I am concerned that our obsession with measuring and simplicity is robbing us of our ability to think and decide for ourselves what is of value. In particular it is leading us to oversimplify and undervalue human intelligence, and to value artificial intelligence inappropriately" (p. 2). Luckin notes that we are overly impressed by machines mainly "because we undervalue what it means to be human" (p. 62). The beauty of using AI is that it can free up educators to focus their attention on deeper learning, including the provision of continuous assessment of each individual's progress toward each goal (Luckin, p. 121). Similarly, we believe that we have failed to develop our social intelligence relative to the broader agenda of what kind of education young people need for the rest of the 21st century. We will show in the vignette at the end of this chapter how AUHSD uses a particular technology to capture the performance of students in real time on their 5Cs, generating a portfolio of performance that they can take into life as they leave secondary school.

We will make the case in Chapter 5 that the professional growth of teachers—*their social intelligence if you will*—has been hampered by the way in which the teaching profession has evolved. Starting with teaching as "the lonely profession" in the one-room schoolhouse 200 years ago, it has often been limited by forms of professional learning that were little more than contrived collegiality (Hargreaves & Fullan, 2012), and stripped of dignity by standardized tests and unrelenting bureaucratic demands. "The system" has squandered the greatest potential social intelligence on the planet: teachers working with each other, students, parents, and community members—and with administrators at the school, district, and maybe even state levels—devoted to the humanity paradigm! And yes, these conditions have brought out some of the worst in teachers and their leaders. It is time to change the tune (see Chapter 5).

Believe it or not, little of this seems to be intended. Most policy makers, and certainly teachers and their leaders that we know, don't like the status quo either. They are stuck in a culture that has been handed down generation after generation. System culture is damn hard to change. It just may be possible to push for the right changes at this time. We believe the majority of every group may be in favor of the changes, once they experience them. The bottom line is that quantum changes in social intelligence, aided by machines, could be our savior. Currently only a few districts, like Anaheim, have figured out how to be successful—despite the system. More would open the floodgates if we could reposition the drivers.

We recognize that there are power blocks to the possibilities we are suggesting. But once underway, we believe that the combination of ideas (the new drivers in action) and power (people at all levels who know that major transformation is needed) will create the social movement needed. Once underway, it will be very hard to stop.

The practical implications relative to our drivers' theme are enormous. We don't need to take a back seat to AI. We need to team up and enter the arena of using AI and other forms of machine intelligence to, on the one hand, free up the time of students and teachers doing drudgery and, on the other hand, to use the new time to further *in concrete ways* the agenda of the humanity paradigm. Because there is no blue-print, some of us will have to take the first steps to learn how to do this, spreading the lessons widely as we help mobilize success. The AUHSD vignette at the end of this chapter is a prime example of taking these calculated steps forward to integrate Social and Machine Intelligence to improve the life chances of young people. In making fundamental reforms, no one in the system questioned what AUHSD was doing, nor did AUHSD leaders ask for permission. In Chapter 5 we will suggest that the policy level should be more proactive in partnering with the middle and local levels.

Before we turn to the Anaheim case, we should cite another reason for being optimistic about a possible fast take up in this direction that we noted in Chapter 1, namely, "6 Reasons Why We Should See Students as Changemakers" (Fullan, 2022). Our good colleague Marc Prensky has been working on the theme of liberating students so they can learn better and deeper. In his new book *Empowered! Re-framing "Growing up" for a New Age*, Prensky (2022) frames the solution, as we do, in terms of the fate and future of humanity. We have evolved, he speculates, "From the 'best species,' created from an ideal image, To a 'big destructive amoeba' starting on the planet Earth, devouring anything in its path, and looking only to grow" (p. 264). We are "not a very self-aware creature . . . humanity is willing to eat and destroy anything in its path, including all other species of animal and plant, and even the planet's existence—in order to keep growing" (p. 264).

If Prensky is right, what is our best bet for turning this around? You know our answer. The cultivation and mobilization of the very young. Those born in 2000 forward are the first generation to have grown up digitally. That is the only world they know. They are potentially the best technologists around. They have both a short and longer time perspective. They want a bigger role. They will need to grow into that role. Those in deep poverty and victims of discrimination will need to be helped out of the deep holes that we have allowed to evolve. If we can help them transcend these challenged beginnings, many of them may turn out to be the best change agents around.

We have already said that *the new purpose of education must focus on individual, community, and societal development that benefits all.* The teaming of the young and old devoted to this agenda, comfortably linked to the as-of-yet limitless power of machines—AI—and more may be just what our best future needs. We will need, as Luckin argues, to teach "beyond the routine cognitive processing of academic subject matter to encompass all elements in an interwoven intelligence model" (p. 95).

The teaming of the young and old devoted to this agenda, comfortably linked to the as-of-yet limitless power of machines— AI—and more may be just what our best future needs.

ACTION GUIDELINES FOR SOCIAL AND MACHINE INTELLIGENCE

- List the connections you see between Driver 2: Social and Machine Intelligence and Driver 1: Well-Being and Learning.

- What has the COVID experience taught you about the Dos and Don'ts of Learning?

- Brainstorm with the community and school how loss of learning may be best addressed in the context of Social and Machine Intelligence.

- Consider how the ideas of this chapter, and the case of Anaheim, can be used to craft an initial action plan.

Anaheim Union High School District is one of the recent entities to join our Deep Learning partnership, having started down this pathway on their own in 2014. They have come very far in a short period of time because they have mobilized youth, accessed and developed amazing technology, and accomplished things that even they had no idea could and should be attempted. The more they know, the more they want to do and the more they want to expand their sphere of interaction beyond Anaheim. AUHSD is a regular public school district in California—one of almost a thousand districts totaling 5.5 million students spread across the state's fifty-eight counties. We examine how they have explicitly integrated human and machine intelligence into crafting new pathways for students to thrive.

Driver 2 Vignette

Anaheim Union
High School District

How has Anaheim Union High School District (AUHSD) as a system been able to harness the power of innovation and technology while using social intelligence to relentlessly focus on positively impacting the humanity of all students and their communities? How are they able to make transformative change when so many districts and schools are locked into the status quo?

AUHSD is one of many school districts in California that consists only of secondary schools, with twenty schools and some 28,000 students. The district's journey of transformation began a decade ago, with a board that had a philosophy of supporting the whole child. However, seven police shootings in 2012, mostly involving the Latinx community, triggered a riot and great tension over the lack of voice in community decisions. When Mike Matsuda became superintendent in 2014 he was already a highly experienced and respected leader in the district with strong instructional expertise. He began to offer Restorative Circles with groups of students. He listened to groups of young people who were turned off by education and who were turning to drugs, gangs, and violence. They pointed out that they needed a pathway to real jobs, mentorships, and apprenticeships. Matsuda and colleagues began with Driver 1 by restoring well-being and setting the stage for new learning.

The district had already adopted the 4Cs of collaboration, creativity, critical thinking, and communication. The students were insightful in identifying two issues. First, they noted that the current 4Cs could be used for good or bad, citing that the Nazis demonstrated the same 4Cs as did many of the local AUHSD drug leaders. So, the 4Cs would not be enough to change their lives or community. Second, they saw some kids make it on to college but they noted they were doing it for themselves and not coming back or improving lives in the community. So, the students brainstormed and agreed that what was missing was a fifth C that combined character and compassion (basically this brings Well-Being linked to Learning into play). The district adopted the fifth C and a belief that all learning needs to be guided by the internal qualities of character, including integrity, and the external application of compassion in contributing back to the community and society.

What developed over the next eight years is an approach that is comprehensive, complex, and multifaceted on the one hand, and is *coherent, deeply, and widely embraced by the whole community* on the other hand. It is innovative, devoted to the well-being and future of students, and supported by all constituencies within the district. It is partnered with key agencies external to the district, including civic bodies, postsecondary institutions, community agencies, and leading-edge businesses. It is clearly "owned" by the internal AUHSD community.

We asked Superintendent Matsuda to capture the key components of their strategy and journey, and he shared this note.

> AUHSD has liberated its students, teachers, and families from the wasteful practice of chasing higher test scores by educating students for purposeful life. The Career Preparedness Systems Framework (CPSF) is a call to action to fulfill a promise too long deferred—to educate the whole child. Beyond a philosophy and conceptual framework, the CPSF is a blueprint for integrating Technical Skills with 21st Century Skills to elevate youth voice and guide students toward their calling or purpose. The CPSF requires a comprehensive, systemic approach to changing the status quo in schools and districts. It begins with a vision.

The vision in AUHSD is that every student will graduate knowing the work that he or she would like to do in the community after high school and the capacity to engage in that work. This is what the district means by students knowing their purpose. A student's purpose might lead him or her to work after graduation, to community college possibly combined with work, or to four-year university. Achieving the vision requires knowing the students, their assets, and their needs, then providing instructional programs that build on strengths and address gaps. A laser focus on empowering students is found in the ubiquitous district catchphrase, *Unlimited You*.

Although they go to school in the shadow of "The Happiest Place on Earth," i.e., Disneyland, nearly 75% of AUHSD's 28,000 students come from low-income families, nearly 6% are homeless, and over 20% are English learners. Thus, a very high proportion of AUHSD students are typically marginalized in US school systems. To achieve the AUHSD vision requires fulfilling the mission to take students from the margins and place them at the center of the educational experience where they can find and elevate their voice as they discover their purpose. The vision and mission define an important role for affective development of every student to prepare them to thrive in life beyond high school. AUHSD succeeds in educating students in terms of Technical Skills, outperforming most California school districts with similar demographics on state-mandated tests, even without emphasizing test preparation or using benchmark assessments.

The 5Cs

Academic programs are strong, but they are not always accessible to all students because of lack of readiness for some students to take certain courses. To build 21st century skills, AUHSD integrates the 5Cs—communication, collaboration, critical thinking, creativity, and compassion—into classroom teaching so that they are working to make new knowledge their own, rather than merely having it delivered to them. As students apply the 5Cs to their learning of chemistry, US history, Algebra II, or any number of electives, they enhance their academic ability while achieving affirmation of their contributions to a classroom community. Combining 21st century skills with technical skills helps students learn the critical process of socially constructing knowledge and helps them to make that knowledge accessible on an ongoing basis as they progress through school. Yet, anyone who has worked with adolescents even for a short period of time understands that seeing the relevance of content and school in general is often a very big challenge. Students require authentic assignments and classroom experiences that engage them with the world beyond school boundaries for them to figure out what they wish to accomplish with their developing skill sets. The more they can explore and understand causes such as health care, diet, or the digital divide, the more likely they are to find a personal mission and to be able to express that mission by speaking out. These experiences start in the classroom with project-based learning and opportunities to communicate with peers about personal learning and passion. But that is not where the experience ends.

Partnerships

More than ninety corporate and nonprofit partners bring the world of work and community striving to students collectively and individually. The Anaheim Innovative Mentoring Experience (AIME) gives students the chance to learn about careers from speakers, engage in mentoring from experts in fields of interest, and work in internships in their senior year to gain real-world experience and imagine how they might fulfill their purpose after high school. AIME engages students in professional and technical worlds normally closed off to them because of immigrant status, poverty, learning differences, or language barriers. AUHSD has taken down the walls between schools and the community to strengthen both. Students are prepared to take full advantage of AIME when entering career and technical education pathways available at all the district's twenty-one schools. The high schools offer between five and eleven multicourse pathways that are often cotaught with community college professors who have expertise beyond the high school faculty. Pathways range from the more traditional, such as food service and hospitality, to newer fields, such as drone technology, cybersecurity, and artificial intelligence. Perhaps most unusual is a pathway to spark innovation called the AUHSD Incubator Lab, open to students across the district. One student, Anthony, exemplifies the importance of pathways coupled with AIME. As a senior, he was enrolled in the cybersecurity pathway and he took a related college-level course. At the same time, he was accepted into an AIME internship in which he worked at a local cybersecurity company. They hired him to work full time after high school graduation, starting at $65,000, and three years later he earns six figures while attending community college at night. His journey to a purposeful life in which he and his family can thrive has begun.

A strong feature of these partnerships in Anaheim is that they link high school experience to career paths in postsecondary institutions with better access to new types of occupations that are being developed in industries. In this way, many career jobs start in high school and carry on after graduation.

Community Schools Approach

As extensive as the career pathways are, they are not sufficient to ensure that all students will develop 21st century and technical skills to the extent they can thrive in the world beyond high school. AUHSD therefore provides numerous programs to help students along their journey of discovery. At a foundational level, the Community Schools program ensures that students and their families have a safety net. But well beyond the typical Community School, the problems and challenges embedded in the neighborhood or city are part of the Community School curriculum so that students learn and experience how they might become part of one or more solutions. Democracy Schools teach students about how to become engaged in civic life at the local level and beyond. Soapbox talks allow students in Democracy Schools to convey a message to their peers, families, and community members about the issues of greatest importance to them and what actions they intend to take to address them. Students wishing to accelerate their way through college to a career can engage in an extensive program of concurrent enrollment in which they earn high school and college credits simultaneously.

Equity in Action

All of the AUHSD programs embedded in the CPSF represent equity in action. When a student such as Anthony who started out as an English learner and was hired into what he considers a dream job, or Alaysia who went from her artificial intelligence pathway in pursuit of computer science at MIT, we are witnessing social mobility for students who in various ways have been kept out of the best education school districts have to offer. The CPSF is a remarkable educational reform that relies on the hard work and innovation of educators throughout the AUHSD system. Superintendent Matsuda strives to have administrators understand the systemic nature of educational change while providing effective support for teachers to improve their practices. It is in classrooms where the CPSF takes hold, and it requires a different kind of teaching. To generate the kinds of educational experiences that elevate student voice and purpose, Matsuda has provided part-time coaches at every school site and curriculum experts based in the central office who work with sites to structure learning consistent with career and technical education pathways, Community Schools, Democracy Schools, and numerous other initiatives. All participate in extensive professional learning that ranges from district workshops to job-embedded analysis and action. AUHSD is committed to providing the kind of support and learning that teachers need to achieve the promise of the CPSF.

> As with any comprehensive initiative in a system as large as AUHSD, the CPSF has been built in pieces over time. Creating programs in schools and nurturing partnerships in the community takes time, persistence, and maximum relationship building. With patience, sustained focus, and political savviness, educators across North America can change what secondary education means in the lives of students.

As we examine the AUHSD experience, it is evident that leadership by Superintendent Matsuda, his district leadership team, and the board have intentionally ensured that Well-Being and Learning (Driver 1) was the mobilizing force that focused and grounded all decisions. Simultaneously, Social Intelligence coupled with technology (Driver 2) was an amplifier as the district built relevant pathways and fostered shared partnership and ownership within the AUHSD community. The district has also partnered with a technology company, e-Kadence, where together they have developed a learning platform to assess the 5Cs in real time linked to pedagogy and assessment of outcomes during and at the end of high school.

AUHSD has fostered a powerful "we-we" sense of pride and accomplishment among the community and students. The list of actual accomplishments is truly astonishing. They are long in number, widely "owned," varied but cohesive, and characterized by actions where the internal ownership and external dividing lines become seamless. The process was to first build the internal capacity to innovate, and then support increasing codevelopment with the internal community and external partners.

One of the first courageous steps was to acknowledge that standardized tests are but one data point in time and then to encourage and support teachers to unleash their energy to design applied learning that was relevant to real life. Massive professional learning opportunities have been focused on the 5Cs and providing the expertise to create relevant applied learning. The teachers created a rubric around the 5Cs so that as students go from classroom to classroom, the learning is not random. Their 5C approach:

- Propels engagement

- Ensures intentional focus on the social-emotional aspects of learning

- Is rooted in inquiry

- Has reached enough penetration that there is consistency across the school

- Has become a new lens for students to look at teachers and at themselves as learners in partnership

This focus on applied learning was a gamechanger when the pandemic hit. While many districts were scrambling to get devices, AUHSD collaborated with its teacher union to support the professional learning of 1,300 teachers to use the online standards so they could design learning focused on engagement and community. The result was applied, relevant learning and higher attendance rates than surrounding districts.

A cornerstone of this relevancy is a core commitment to civic engagement for which the district leads the state in The Seal of Civic Engagement. A few of the programs that foster civic engagement and opportunities for all to succeed include:

- The Anaheim Pledge among several colleges and the district for the benefit of new scholars among its students.

- Career and technical education pathways and dual enrollment to all sites in trending fields, such as cybersecurity, biomedical, biodata, and AI.

- Creation of the Magnolia Agriscience Community Center, an urban community farm investigating the issue of food deserts in urban communities; this has important implications for food supplies and poverty (we return to the multifaceted importance of the urban farm in Chapter 6).

- Six California School Boards Association Golden Bell Awards in the past six years for model programs in language acquisition and dual language immersion (Spanish, Vietnamese).

- Creation of an innovation lab with partners so that students can bring their ideas to action. There are so many issues, from housing, violence, and drugs to climate change. Students are trying to solve these problems and are encouraged to go beyond simply researching issues or suggesting solutions but to become more entrepreneurial by identifying ways they can make their solutions a reality. This lines up with the district lens of their fifth C (character and compassion) and the district vision to create a better world through the "Unlimited You." The belief is that your ideas are going to move the needle of social justice and contribute to the common good.

- AIME, a business-district partnership that provides mentorship and internships so that all students may experience multiple career options by exposing them to mentorships with business, medical, and community personnel who can share their perspectives. This is an intentional strategy to provide access and opportunity to students whose circumstances may not include family friends or relatives who can open doors.

AUHSD is actively addressing the need for new assessments to match the 5Cs and their vision for students who will thrive personally and contribute to the world. They have developed a Capstone Framework to support schools in designing performance assessments that provide a much more comprehensive picture of what students know and are able to do. Students present their learning to panels of business leaders, teachers, and community members. This alternative assessment that measures what matters is being recognized by their partners in higher ed.

Anaheim demonstrates the nuance of Driver 2—integrating Social and Machine Intelligence. They have integrated a relentless focus on putting students at the center of all decisions while fostering powerful relationships (social intelligence) with exploiting the best of technology trends and resources to amplify life chances for their students (machine intelligence). This is manifested as they listen to students and parents and involve them in decisions while simultaneously creating career pathways such as cybersecurity and artificial intelligence that prepare students to move into emerging fields.

Finally, in a recent dramatic fashion, AUHSD's school board proved our point that school districts can be system players. The State of California assesses progress of its schools with an annual dashboard that has eight indicators (Grade 11 English and Math, Advanced Placement exams, and other academic measures). As of February 2023, the board has a draft School Board Resolution to add a ninth indicator to the California College/Career (CCI) dashboard. This indicator is none other than our Global Competencies (they don't have "character" and do have "compassion," which we have recently added as part of character). One of the clauses in their proposal reads as follows:

> Whereas: California's current academic success measures paint an incomplete picture of students' career and college readiness because vital career and life skills like critical thinking, collaboration, creativity, communication, compassion, and civic engagement are not included in the College/Career Readiness state dashboard.

The board motion then proposes "A ninth College and Career Readiness Indicator allowing a district to use a locally adopted graduate student profile/capstone as a recognized completion metric under the College and Career Indicators (CCI)"—a measure that the board has already developed and tested.

At a time when traditional academic measures are widely seen as insufficient, or even wrong (narrow testing), it is a school board that is stepping in to fill the gap, offering to share its learnings with others!

At AUHSD, the four drivers work in concert. While the Social and Machine Intelligence is evident, we see the other three drivers having a strong impact. The combination of the 5Cs' focus on applied, relevant learning with the array of opportunities to build a pathway to future careers and advanced learning clearly addresses Driver 1 by impacting wellness and learning but simultaneously exemplifies Equity-Equality Investments (Driver 3). The constellation of partnerships and focus between the district, business, and community are addressing inequities through quality investments of time, funding, and human resources. The impact is changing the lives of students like Anthony and so many more. The result is a phenomenally wide and deep set of learning pathways that are getting results over a remarkably brief period. This is what we mean by Systemness (Driver 4) and what we call a "go slow to go fast" strategy.

> *The result is a phenomenally wide and deep set of learning pathways that are getting results over a remarkably brief period.*

COHERENCE MAKING

Fullan had the opportunity to write the foreword to a new book about to be published by David Brazer and Michael Matsuda (in press) titled *Education for a Purposeful Life*. This is the first sentence of the foreword: "Students attending and graduating from AUHSD make Anaheim City a better place to live!" Although we are just seeing partial success, higher proportions of all students from disadvantaged backgrounds, including the 1,650 homeless among its 28,000 total, do better and have increased life chances for themselves. They do this in a way that they make for better citizens while they are in school and after they graduate. We have not seen a careful study, but our hypothesis would be the school system makes students better, who in turn make the city better in terms of production of companies, improvement of community life, safety, longevity, and overall happiness. Wow! The value and productivity of business enterprises, their social value to the city, especially with respect to high-tech companies, has—potentially—increased exponentially. They are not only ready for any army of Chatbots—whether they be called ChatGPT, Bard (Google), Claude (Anthropic), ERNIE (Baidu), or whatever—but they are also ready to use them for the further development of humanity. Review the large number of video vignettes produced by AUHSD and you will find diverse students and adults working together who possess an articulate shared understanding of the nature of Deep Learning that permeates their learning. The kind of Deep Learning that sticks with you for a long time as graduates become lifelong learners.

Our hypothesis would be the school system makes students better, who in turn make the city better in terms of production of companies, improvement of community life, safety, longevity, and overall happiness.

The teaming of humans and machines will grow exponentially over the next period as we learn to leverage AI's growing capacity. We also see that regular school districts, like AUHSD, can be in the driver's seat (sorry, this is the only time we will use this pun). AUHSD exercises this right without any extra legitimacy or help from the state. They just do it! And we would say they are all the more admired for it. Imagine if the state deliberately helped with Driver 3 (Equity-Equality Investments) and Driver 4 (Systemness) as the board contributes to the state's need to improve outcome measurement.

Local groups are not used to thinking about being "system players," but that is exactly where we are heading in the next two chapters. The world view of locals (students, teachers, parents, school leaders, community members, regional leaders) needs to be expanded. Locals *are* the system.

In the meantime, massive potential amounts of social intelligence have been squandered over the years.

Driver 3: Equity-Equality Investments

4 SYSTEMNESS

1 WELL-BEING AND LEARNING

Coherence Making

2 SOCIAL AND MACHINE INTELLIGENCE

Denotes the development of resources to support equity (fairness of initial investment in developing people and society) that produce greater equality (outcomes that reduce the gap among individuals and groups of people) and increase prosperity for all.

3

Elements

- Supporting macro Equity-Equality strategies, such as tax reform, poverty reduction, job creation, fair wages, mental and physical health, community development, career paths, early childhood, and the like

- Engaging in local Equity-Equality practices: community schools, family health centers, homelessness, food, shelter, and safety

CHAPTER 4

Driver 3
Equity-Equality Investments

D river 3 concerns investments in society and local entities that would improve or develop the core aspects of living that would produce and support a quality system (Driver 4). The question is: What and how does society invest in Well-Being and Learning (Driver 1), social and artificial intelligence (Driver 2), and Equity-Equality system change (Driver 3)? We would want to know how much society invests in these domains, and how wisely, in order to get desired results. The investments in the other drivers become part and parcel of Equity-Equality Investments for the system as a whole. For our purposes, *equality* means the state of being equal and *equity* adds the element of justice or fairness. Equal treatment does not produce equity, nor does it produce equality when conditions and circumstances are very different. One can think of equity as the process of investing in development and equality as the desired outcome. We use the term *Equity-Equality Investments* to denote the need for resources to achieve greater equality of outcomes. We are focused on both inputs and outputs. We also recognize that radical inequality is fundamental to the history of colonial societies and is extremely difficult to alter. Substantial progress will have to be the marker of success.

EQUITY-EQUALITY
INVESTMENTS FOR ALL

Equity starts with fairness, and there is no question that most systems are deeply inequitable with prejudice running from blatant and persistent racism, to other inequities that are more hidden. We hold one other key premise: The world can afford to support the basic needs and goals of all its 8 billion people. Poverty is evil, destructive of all, and unnecessary given our worldwide resources. Helping people flourish in relation to the tripartite goals of self, community, and society is good for all. Our dynamic world of the future need not be a zero-sum proposition. In fact, the opposite is true: In the evolving future we all prosper or none of us do. You might be shocked to learn that billions on trillions of dollars have been spent in Western society on equity since World War II with only an initial blip forward for two decades (1950 to 1970 or so). There has been some reduction of extreme poverty in relation to food, but overall we have seen a substantial and ever-increasing downward decline in equality for the past fifty years. We will present the data shortly, but for now, we offer the conclusion that equity has failed because its investment has been *siloed*. Put another way, equity investments have ignored the drivers as a set and thus have had little chance of success.

In the evolving future we all prosper or none of us do.

AUSTERITY

Over the past fifty years, the rich have been able to reap massive percentages of profit while lower- and middle-class fortunes have plummeted in Western societies. On a world-wide basis, the percentage of people going to bed hungry decreased until about 2015 and since then increased to about 9%. About 690 million are chronically undernourished (www.weforum.org). To remind our readers about the bias in the distribution of money exposed by economists, the basic problem is that the gross domestic product, which has been the measure of economic growth, is structured in such a way that the "owners" (capitalists) reap the lion's share of profits, while the workers get comparatively tiny amounts.

Between 1980 and 2016 (and still going) the bottom 90% of income earners experienced income growth that was slower than the national average (in other words, higher income earners received the lion's share), and so on. Boushey (2019) documents how income, wealth, and mobility interact. Higher incomes can be saved in stock, which in turn makes investments possible that yield more wealth to those who already have the money. The effects of these trends can be calculated in different ways (all favoring the rich). For example, from 1980 to 2007, the income share of the top 1% expanded from 9.4% to 27.6% of total wealth. Mazzucato (2018, p. 4) reports that by 2015 the combined wealth of the sixty-two richest people in the world was about the same as the bottom half of the world's population—3.5 billion people. This situation and trend is destructive for the future health and survival of society, possibly in our lifetimes.

OPPORTUNITIES FOR TRANSFORMATION

New, substantial Equity-Equality Investments are the essence of Driver 3. It's clearest if we divide investments into two types. We have already documented that the macroeconomic fundamentals favors the very rich while punishing those at the bottom and middle. In a moment we will make the case that this situation is not good for the rich either, but let's first address those at the bottom, where we find lower life expectancy and lives of discrimination and prejudice. We know that, during the pandemic, minorities and low-income individuals suffered significantly more than those who were well-off. In these cases, equality investments are often essential for survival. The macroeconomic policies that are required include revamping income tax and related mechanisms that currently favor the rich, guaranteed minimum income that subsidizes low-income individuals, universal access to high-quality daycare, minimum wages, subsidized daycare, medical and health benefits, housing assistance, and so on. At the macro level, this work may lead to urban developments that benefit low-income people and provide opportunities for mobility. This work on altering macroeconomics must continue.

We know that, during the pandemic, minorities and low-income individuals suffered significantly more than those who were well-off.

Health economists Richard Wilkinson and Kate Pickett (2019) in their book *Inner Level* show that large income gaps between the rich and the poor "damage us all." Reductions in inequality "not only reduce the burden of health and social problems throughout society, but also dramatically improve both the psychological well-being and the quality of social relations that are essential to health and happiness" (p. xi). Moreover, with large gaps we are less likely to cooperate with respect to climate threats, and related crises. On almost every dimension inequality is negatively associated with less healthy societies overall.

We have said that equity has failed because it has been siloed as a separate problem. The reason we should not want equity siloed is not only about justice, but rather because when we integrate equity and equality, everyone gains. We also enter a very complex set of change problems. The nuances about getting equality and equity right are complex but essential to overall success. We see this clearly in our vignettes. When we consider the three dimensions of purpose (self, community, and society) we fail every time if we don't tackle differences. In brief, in our current situation, addressing social justice and saving society from multifaceted destruction are one and the same.

We also have new insight into inequity and inequality. First, it is clear that it is a pervasive system problem involving both Drivers 3 and 4 (and these two drivers, by definition, cascade downward to Drivers 1 and 2). And Drivers 1 and 2 affect 3 and 4 for better or for worse. We need the system of the four drivers working in concert. Ignoring differences, or shrugging off problems in today's world, is a recipe for disaster. Our knowledge base and the degrees of anxiety about the problems we face are now at a level where new action is required. More bold, extensive transformational attempts are coming to the fore. Much more is needed. We argue here that investing in all four drivers is both essential and impactful.

As in the previous two chapters, we start with some brief guidelines that might initiate the driver.

ACTION GUIDELINES FOR EQUITY-EQUALITY INVESTMENTS

- Define the purpose and vision of the change you would like to see.

- Recognize that the time is ripe for bold action—be ambitious, find kindred spirits.

- Consider what will you change at the school level. What needs to change outside of the school?

- Define the scope of the initiative in terms of those who will be affected.

- Develop the strategy jointly with others, both those who benefit and those who suffer from the status quo.

- Constantly define, revise, and communicate the strategy as you go.

- Assess and review measurable progress on a continuous basis, celebrating success and digging deeper with respect to seemingly intractable problems.

As before, we will use a case example to portray actual attempts at system or subsystem levels to bring about change—transformation, actually—that illustrate the potential of the new era in action. The case in question is San Diego County in California where an initiative is under-way to decrease poverty and increase learning on a very large scale.

We work with the San Diego County Office of Education (SDC), which oversees and supports forty-three school districts serving more than 500,000 students, and operates one of those forty-three districts which directly serves incarcerated individuals, homeless students, foster youth, pregnant teens, and migrants. SDC is committed to reducing poverty by 33% over the next seven years. To be successful, SDC will need to significantly reduce poverty and increase Well-Being and Learning on a scale not yet attempted. The work will be enabled potentially by the major new investment in California of $4.1 billion to support the development of a new conception of Community Schools.

The SDC represents a fantastic, deliberate transformational goal that has never before been undertaken on this scale. Frankly, nobody really knows how to do this in detail, although the county superintendent, Paul Gothold, led a smaller district a decade ago engaged in similar developments. We offer the case as a harbinger of what is to come in the near future— serious, specific commitments to implement Driver 3, using explicit Equity-Equality Investments connected to the other three drivers, along with Deep Learning focused on whole system transformation. We outline the plan so far, noting that implementation has just begun as we write this so we can only capture the initial thinking and strategy.

Driver 3 Vignette

San Diego County

Driver 3 concerns *investments in society and local entities that would improve or develop the core aspects of living to produce and support a quality living system.* The challenge is how society can and should act to get the desired results, which is to move more than 75,000 students out of poverty while increasing the quality of learning. To be successful, SDC will need an approach that combines strategies to significantly reduce poverty by impacting nonschool poverty factors, such as homelessness, food insecurity, and jobs, while also increasing Well-Being and Learning. Improving neighborhoods while improving schools must be done synergistically.

The Challenge

How do you transform the life chances of thousands of students and the trajectory of a whole community? That is the question that the San Diego County Office of Education (SDC) has taken on. Superintendent Paul Gothold and his leadership team recognized that they were serving forty-three school districts and 500,000 students in a region where half the households earn less than $35,000 per year for a family of four. Traditionally, county education offices provide support and oversee policy compliance to schools and districts—in this case, forty-three school districts—whereas this new goal consists of coconstructing a joint solution among county, district, and community agencies with active participation of students, teachers, and parents.

Unique Qualifications

Gothold has some experience on a much smaller scale in reducing poverty and improving life chances during his leadership when he was superintendent in the Lynwood Unified School District (just outside Los Angeles).

In the period from 2010 to 2017, the Lynwood district

- Convened a large group of constituents that included the mayor, chamber of commerce, bargaining chairs, district/site administrative representatives, students, parents, and community members to develop a strategic plan for the district that would guide their work for the next five years.

- Established space to cocreate opportunities with the community based on listening to their desires and needs. This led to the creation of a school-based community health center open to anyone for primary care; working with thirty-two health agencies; and universal screening so every child had access to these services along with mental health, vision, dental, and more.

- Developed pathways for parent employment within and outside the district. One example through adult education was the creation of an LVN certificate program to satisfy the demand for skilled labor at the local hospital.

- Redefined all elective offerings for children based on the demand for skilled labor and student interest (for example, biotech, engineering, construction trades, health pathways, computer science, and arts media pathways). All options were created with higher education and industry professionals and resulted in students' ability to obtain college credit while in high school as well as certification to enter directly into the workforce.

- Ensured every course, both core and electives, were A-G (a designation in the California school system that a course meets academic standards) approved so that every student graduating was eligible to apply for a four-year program if they opted to do so.

- Eliminated tracking to create heterogeneous grouping before twelfth grade so that expectations for every child/grade level/content were the same and with supports varying depending on the needs of each individual student.

- Eliminated all prerequisites, creating open access for any students to participate in Advanced Placement (AP) or International Baccalaureate (IB) courses. As a result, participation tripled, passage rates went up, and Lynwood was identified as AP College Board District of the Year for midsized districts, a national recognition.

These strategies led to Lynwood Unified graduation rates increasing from 58% in 2010 to more than 90% in every comprehensive high school by 2017. The district is currently 94.3% Hispanic and Latinx, 4.47% Black, and 1.23% other. That dramatic increase included the four-year cohort graduating with no gaps in any student population subgroup. The district also experienced the highest growth in the state on California tests two years in a row. Although Lynwood did not focus on Deep Learning per se, Superintendent Gothold brings this experience to lead the aspirational change in San Diego County.

It takes a team effort to effect such transformational change, and the county has direct experience in effecting this change in the school district it leads. This "county-led" district serves students who are incarcerated, expelled, homeless, foster youth, pregnant/teen mothers/fathers, migrants, refugees, and any other population who have been historically under-served. County leaders have created unique learning opportunities that serve as a model for districts who want to transform both learning and life chances. One example is the Youth in Custody program. Their approach to dealing with youth who may be angry, disengaged, or without hope has been to change the *learning environment*. While the norm is to create custodial sites with very strict rules, instead they created a Youth Transition Center. The center focuses on a rich outdoor environment and offers college credit courses, performing arts, and community-organized partnerships for job placement and housing. They focus on celebrating small wins throughout the year and supporting graduates along the way with innovations, such as their breaking-barriers newsletter. And it works. The county began with 620 incarcerated youth and has reduced that number to 120 over the past five years. This attention to community factors combined with authentic, engaged learning has shown it gets results and will inform the next stages of the journey.

More recently, during the pandemic, SDC became a contractor to raise millions of dollars to bring internet services to more than 77,000 students and families. It is this contextual literacy that will support SDC to collaboratively identify needs and coconstruct solutions with their communities.

Mobilizing for Action

The strategy to influence transformation across the forty-two districts SDC supports has two components: internal development and transformed relationships with external partners.

Internal Development

Step 1. Develop Internal Goals, Capacity, and Ownership

The first step was to get their own leadership in order. To propel the internal development the executive leadership team challenged themselves to change their internal capacity, organization, and ownership of the strategy. Ownership, purpose, and goals were framed by asking the question: "What would it look like if private, public, and philanthropic groups worked together in harmony to best support the well-being and success of every child?" The result of that process was an articulation of the belief that a unique opportunity exists by reimagining the school as the central hub for community transformation that could lead to new learning by building on existing assets and creating new opportunities for every family unit and child.

Step 2. Articulate the Shift in Organizational Practice: The Equity Blueprint

Leadership recognized that to become a transformational organization they must shift from a compliance orientation to an innovation orientation. This represents an essentially different model of providing assistance as coaches and influencers rather than compliance makers.

They developed an Equity Blueprint to frame the work they would do together as a team and with external partners.

As stated in SDC's Equity Blueprint,

> [I]n order to fulfill our collective promise of meeting the Board's four goals – Career Tech Ed., Equity, Innovation and Organizational Effectiveness, we commit to reducing the number of students who qualify for free or reduced lunch from 49% to 35% by 2027. We will do this by:

> - Ensuring Active **Family and Community Engagement** by partnering with families to create successful outcomes for students.

> - **Integrating Students Support**, *including high-quality teaching and learning*, so that each student has what they need to thrive in and out of school.

> - Offering **Expanded and Enriched Learning Opportunities** to cultivate a love for learning and a pathway to careers and future community success.

> - Engaging in **Collaborative Leadership Practices** where each educational partner embraces shared responsibility to one another's success.

This articulation described a new approach of listening, capturing the voices of those they serve, and then coconstructing solutions. Internally they are moving from developing siloed solutions within departments to crafting integrated approaches that provide cohesive strategy as a team and are aligned with the Equity Blueprint. One early example is led by the Leadership and Learning Division, which has provided leadership to districts in the early work of developing portraits of a learner, the educator, and the system. This cross-department team is currently developing their capacity as facilitators of Deep Learning and the community school context. Note our caution in this case example: It refers to "preliminary plans that are just being formulated." It is based on the findings that as students develop the competencies they need to flourish in life this directly lifts them from poverty over time. Simultaneously, the county offers a range of educational opportunities for adults to increase their employability with new skills and certifications to meet market trends. This learning focus is crucial but must be augmented in collaboration with a robust business and community strategy.

Engaging External Partnerships

SDC has embraced a socially conscious leadership stance to mobilize the community and its schools to reduce poverty and thus unleash the well-being and success of every child. This is based on a belief in forming deep community relationships and codeveloping local capacity.

SDC has articulated the challenge and the opportunity across multiple groups of families, community members, philanthropists, policymakers, and educators. Their philosophy is guided by civil rights advocate John Powell's definition of poverty:

> In a legitimate democracy, belonging means that your well-being is considered and your ability to help design and give meaning to its structures and institutions is realized. Members are more than just individuals; they also have collective power and share a linked fate. Those who stand outside the community have trouble making claims on it. It is not so much that they cannot speak as it is that they are not likely to be heard. This is what I define

as poverty . . . *Thus an anti-poverty agenda must begin with a new understanding of poverty as being primarily about belongingness and bringing the imagined other back into the sphere of community and the circle of human concern. Creating belongingness will eradicate poverty and eradicating poverty will help create belongingness.* (2012)

When the focus is on building *belongingness* rather than fixing deficits, the strategy shifts. This leads to joint determination of both issues and solutions in a transparent and mutually respectful collaboration.

The SDC theory of action is to

- Build trust through honest feedback and joint work

- Connect with partners and foster deep interaction

- Jointly influence learning, policy, community engagement, and services

This will be facilitated by maintaining an inquiry stance, not a prescriptive one, and by creating conditions that honor human development.

The Strategy

Two strands of focused action are being pursued with external partners simultaneously. The strands are aligned in principles, interconnected, and feed on each other synergistically.

1. Build an Ecosystem of Alliances to Address Nonschool Factors

SDC leaders have engaged with all levels of policymakers, community agencies, philanthropists, government, unions, families, and educators to build shared meaning about the task ahead and to develop commitment to the goal of reducing poverty.

This includes

- Convening regional and national partners to ensure private, public, and nonprofit entities are working in harmony to meet the needs of all students in each school community
- Regularly evaluating/creating policy at local, regional, and state levels to support such efforts
- Leveraging existing relationships with county supervisors and local delegates to create a confluence of efforts around support for healthy school communities
- Being at the table with decision makers at all levels

This meta-level strategy will tackle the nonschool factors of community poverty with local and national partners.

2. Transform Learning in Community Schools

The SDC vision of Community Schools goes far beyond wraparound services to encompass a new way of learning for all and new forms of partnership with all levels of community so that every child is successful and the community thrives. The intention is to shift the priorities of all schools by mobilizing new Well-Being and Learning within a community school framework of support. SDC will invite and engage districts to assess needs and coconstruct strategic plans that will simultaneously reduce poverty and increase relevant, authentic learning and well-being.

They have created two strategic partnerships to support this work: CSLX (an independent support agency with expertise in Community Schools) and New Pedagogies for Deep Learning with its expertise in Deep Learning.

All forty-two districts have been invited to engage in building shared meaning about how to practically transform learning in a community school context. SDC has hosted capacity building institutes for Community Schools and Deep Learning. Several districts are engaging as cohorts in Deep Learning capacity building. SDC leaders are continuing to build their knowledge and capacity so they can take the stance of coaches, not compliance officers, in this new work.

Measuring Success

The commitment to joint determination and connected autonomy is clear. This means the strategy in detail has to be built with those who are part of the process of coconstruction. This is not work for those who want a predetermined plan. This is messy work.

There will be several indicators to mark progress along the way, including

- Active citizenship and participation in the democratic process in and out of school
- Levels of access to health care (primary, mental, dental, vision) and food/housing
- Healthy kids survey measuring students' belongingness
- Family surveys measuring feelings of connectedness to the school community, inclusion, and restorative practices
- Levels of poverty as measured by free and reduced lunch
- Greater presence of Deep Learning (see Chapter 6) in schools
- More engagement of students in learning and in community projects
- Increased morale of students, staff, and parents

Some of the early actions and strategies reflect a strong commitment to action.

1. Convene collaborators to attack the nonschool factors of poverty and create communities of belonging— where voices are heard and respected as cocreators of solutions. Mobilize communities with partners from policy, philanthropy, government, families, and education to assess needs and create solutions to reduce poverty, housing scarcity, job insecurity, and more.

2. Simultaneously create student-centered schools where authentic engaged learning will help students to identify their passions and skills. Schools become hubs for the

community offering a full range of services for health, wellness, and learning so that youth develop the Global Competencies they need to create a future for themselves as individuals and contributors to their community and society. SDC has begun by supporting schools in their country that have been awarded Community Schools grants. They have been awarded a technical assistance grant to use their expertise to support two additional counties in Southern California. In all cases, their approach is one of joint determination, learning from the work, and diffusing insights.

The crucial variable will be the ability to tackle both nonschool factors and in-school learning to create vibrant communities that build cultures of belonging where every voice is respected, the economic needs of communities are met, and the passions of youth are unleashed. This is a bold venture—the stakes are high—but it's one that is a crucial marker if we are to address inequities, well-being, and learning.

We should note that the forty-two districts within SDC have their own governing school boards that operate independently of SDC. We will be reporting in the near future on our work in other districts such as Vista Unified School District.

We normally only report on case studies that are well underway and have a degree of completion. We make an exception in the SDC case because it is tackling social change on a scale never before attempted and doing so with powerful and specific goals. We will be reporting on its progress in future publications. We don't know whether SDC will be successful, but this is the kind of audacious move we would expect in the serious pursuit of the humanity paradigm.

COHERENCE MAKING

We think the value of the SDC initiative, along with the other case examples in this book, illustrate what should be tried and to a certain extent what could be accomplished. We also think that the rest of this decade—2023 to 2030—could be a transformational period for the role of learning in society. A good emerging example is Scotland's Northern Alliance collaborative. In striving for greater equity, Scotland has organized its system into six regional entities called Regional Improvement Collaboratives or RICs. One of them, The Northern Alliance collaborative, has organized its efforts around the four drivers as a coherence-making endeavor. This has enabled them to develop an active framework that focuses on well-being, collaboration, implementation, and a growing improvement culture (Muir, 2022; Northern Alliance, 2022). Their next step is to go deeper into pedagogy to tie together Well-Being and Learning using focused collaboration linked to achieving greater equitable outcomes. The ongoing reports reflect greater clarity and sense of cohesion among leaders, teachers, and students. We are now talking about a whole country (or at least one-sixth of a coordinated plan), which means that the relationship between the RIC and government policy will be crucial in the next phase.

This, of course, brings us to another driver—Systemness itself—the degree to which people learn and realize there is a system, recognize their place in it, learn about other levels, and are conscious and active about transforming it for the better. Thus, Driver 4 involves the consciousness and involvement of scores of people, especially the young, to realize and act accordingly that *we are all the system!* Systemness is somewhat uncharted territory, but we perceive a growing interest at all levels that overall Systemness should be a concern of everyone.

We perceive a growing interest at all levels that overall Systemness should be a concern of everyone.

Driver 4: Systemness

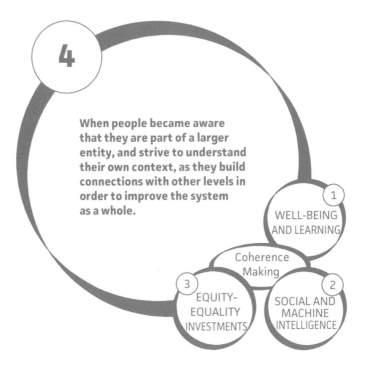

4

When people became aware that they are part of a larger entity, and strive to understand their own context, as they build connections with other levels in order to improve the system as a whole.

1 WELL-BEING AND LEARNING

Coherence Making

3 EQUITY-EQUALITY INVESTMENTS

2 SOCIAL AND MACHINE INTELLIGENCE

Elements

- Enlarging your local sense of identity within your school and community and across schools in the district (networks)

- Considering how schools/community and the district can achieve greater coherence and collective identity

- Fostering a "we-we" identity within your school district/network

- Considering how you can engage the base, mobilize the middle, and intrigue the top

- Rebuilding the system from the ground up with crisscrossing action within and across the levels

CHAPTER 5

Driver 4

Systemness: Everyone's Agenda

We now come to the point where we can ask: "Is it even possible to talk about system change in a practical way?" Systems do change, but not usually by master plans. Big changes are typically a function of the accumulation of historical forces, or because of major disruptions (such as a global pandemic). The question is: Can large-scale transformation be shaped by deliberate efforts of humans working together? We don't really know. We have had some success in improving literacy, numeracy, and high school graduation rates, but this is no longer sufficient. The circumstances and agenda are way more complex. Education changes in the first decade of this century were simpler compared to what we are currently facing. We now find that most students are no longer satisfied to put their time into academic learning as an end in itself. The kinds of problems we are facing require a radically different approach to the old model of system change. We are proposing an alternative model of system change for 2023 and beyond. Systemness that encompasses all levels in co-constructing solutions.

THE EMERGENCE OF SYSTEMS THINKING

We have great respect for systems thinking, chaos theory, and its related formulations. In Chapter 1 we introduced Driver 4 and mentioned the powerful new initiative at MIT with Peter Senge and Mette Böll to develop compassionate system leaders and noted that the program will not develop leaders fast enough to make a big difference (nor is it intended for such a purpose). The lived Systemness we need goes beyond simply a systems-thinking mindset on the part of a few. We need a pervasive commitment to connected action at every level. The good news is that, ironically, the pandemic has made us all aware of the bigger picture. The young in particular are ready to participate in bigger solutions. All four drivers can reinforce and leverage this opportunity with young people. We need to build the new system from the bottom and middle up and across.

Top-down system initiatives often focus on what Fuller and Kim (2022) of the Brookings Institution refer to as standards-based accountability (SBA). After reviewing several examples, the authors conclude, "True to classic systems theory, SBA's contemporary adherents do claim that the organization's goals and means should be defined at the top of the system, with central actors allocating key inputs and guiding the content and pedagogy delivered by teachers—then pressing school-level managers for results" (p. 13).

In this century, top-down system leadership has not resulted in major change except perhaps in the case of basic skills (even that requires skilled leaders at the top). It may sound like we are being unduly critical, but our main point is that deliberate system change is incredibly complex and difficult. The world has become too complex and troubled—with trust at an all-time low—to be run from the top. Instead, we have to help or allow the base and the middle to develop and connect with others latterly and upward. AUHSD (Chapter 3) is one such example. Later in this chapter we will talk about a possible new model that includes all levels—local, middle, and top.

An interesting account of the vagaries of top-down government when it comes to education policy comes from two longtime veterans of English education reform: Mick Waters and Tim Brighouse (2022). The two authors, having been witness to many of the developments they write about, examined the evolution of education reform in England from 1945 to 2021. They interviewed all secretaries of education (the top education minister) who were still alive plus numerous other officials, and also examined scores of official documents. They divided the period into two chunks: the age of optimism and trust (1945 to 1976) and the age of centralization and managerialism (1976 to 2021). Two things stand out in Waters and Brighouse's mammoth 600+ page account. First, one sees two long periods: relative decentralization and later corrective centralization. Second, school people would have experienced a large number of secretaries of education during this seventy-five-year period, with their varying political personalities. There were seventeen different secretaries of education between 1988 and 2021, or a different minister every two years on average (Foundation for Education Development, 2022)!

In short, in addition to being too complex to be run from the top, there is frequent turnover of system leadership. If you are a school leader or teacher, you would be wise not to depend on central leadership for consistency. Let's flip the question on its head and ask how those at lower levels can influence continuity of development and system change. Or, how can we achieve greater Systemness? There is still a role for the top, but we have to get at it from the bottom up.

FORGING GREATER SYSTEMNESS

As a general guideline, we have tried to capture the recent tendencies in our own system thinking (Figure 5.1).

FIGURE 5.1 ● System Orientation

Build the base	**Mobilize the middle**	**Intrigue the top**

Systemness, of course, is a very elusive concept. We define it as practically as possible. It is about oneself—you as a reader—and all relevant things outside you. It is to be *aware, concerned about*, and *involved in* things that are beyond you but in some ways affect your life and the lives of humans more generally. *Systemness is when people in the system become aware that they are part and parcel of a larger entity: their community, district, state, country, world, and universe. They become aware and conscious that there is a bigger system at work, that they should strive to understand it, influence it. Ultimately, in our view,* **everyone has a responsibility with others to improve the system!**

Build the base (students, local communities, schools, principals) is where the heart of innovations must lie. *Mobilize the middle* refers to regional and district entities that must be engaged in enabling roles. *Intrigue the top* is deliberately playful. We need the bottom and middle to innovate, without getting literal permission, doing things that once noticed are found to be intriguing. Those at the top seek to be intrigued. Those innovating don't mind being noticed. In some ways, all five vignettes in this book can be seen as containing elements of the model we are surfacing here. They first worked hard at local development and eventually wanted to be part of wider discussions and developments because they knew the issues were of vital importance for, well, the humanity paradigm.

Below we will provide a profile of a model called the Systemness Model that contains the elements for overall system success. In the meantime, knowing where you reside in the system, knowing other levels of subsystems, and being aware of how the pieces connect and interact are also part of Systemness. For the sake of simplicity let's assume that there are three levels: local school and community, district or region (the middle), and policy level (or top). In federal systems, there are two layers near the top. One order of business for local members and leaders is to learn about their own level—other schools and communities, for example. This is internal collaboration that enables local cohesion. A second order of business is to learn about the layer above you—your district or region. The third and final level is to learn something about the policy level. Reflect on Systemness in your context and use the prompts in Figure 5.2 to record where you fit and how you relate and influence other levels of the system.

> *Knowing where you reside in the system, knowing other levels of subsystems, and being aware of how the pieces connect and interact are also part of Systemness.*

FIGURE 5.2 ● System Levels

		HOW DOES THIS WORK IN YOUR CONTEXT?
1.	**LOCAL: School and Community Members**	
	Who is in this level? What makes them tick?	
	What would it mean to build the base?	
2.	**MIDDLE: District or Region Players**	
	Who is in this level? What makes them tick?	
	What would it take to mobilize the middle?	
3.	**POLICY: Policymakers**	
	Who is in this level? What makes them tick?	
	What would attract policymakers to join in?	

We are not asking that you study each level, only that you are aware of who they are, and maybe what makes them tick. There are three additional concepts that those familiar with our work will know: contextual literacy, empathy, and joint determination. Contextual literacy refers to the degree to which people understand the culture in which they work. Empathy concerns the understanding you have about others within and external to your group. Joint determination consists of enabling day-to-day development and problem solving on the part of those closest to the pain and the potential for success.

When you put it all together you will know that the drivers as a set, and the Deep Learning Framework itself, serve to enable participants to build their Systemness knowledge as they go. When we say that students are changemakers, we are saying that they have a propensity to take into account and to learn more about the contexts—local and otherwise—in which they live. As they go about their work with greater learning and well-being, they are expanding their Systemness knowledge. They become better change agents.

The whole local system becomes more knowledgeable about its own system and connections. For example, when Ottawa goes about its Deep Learning work *they become more system aware.* Their knowledge of the system and its transformation aspirations becomes greater, and, of critical importance, the more it is shared. Similarly, the Anaheim case (Chapter 3) developed over the past nine years reflects growing awareness of and strategies aimed at changing the system and its culture. Much of that does not require formal policy permission. But when they did encounter policy constraints concerning assessment of outcomes, the school board developed a policy proposal (that they are currently in the process of submitting to the state) to add the assessment of their 5Cs as an official, accepted outcome recognized by the state on its dashboard of official outcomes as a ninth official outcome to join the other eight more traditional outcome measures. This is a potential example of system change caused by the middle!

For us, system transformation is one of the main goals. As locals become more knowledgeable about what is needed, they identify with other locals, thereby increasing cohesion. They become more committed and effective in relation to local change while increasing their desire to influence outward and upward. They become players and partners in system change. Read the two vignettes at the end of this chapter—Association of Independent Schools of New South Wales (AISNSW) and the country of Uruguay. In both cases you will see a force for local change and the potential for affecting the system as a whole. After a while, the Systemness of the entity (AISNSW) or whole state (in the case of Uruguay) is positively affected.

Systemness need not be linear or need not come from the top or the bottom, but it will be a function of parts of the system that begin system mobilization. It may take a while to get used to, but in the new more complex situation, promoting Systemness and its connections is everyone's responsibility. In our new model, we have reversed existing top-down thinking and explored what it would mean to build the base (the so-called bottom), mobilize the middle (districts/regions), and intrigue the top (attract policymakers to join in). We expect (predict) more explicit action at the system level in the next period (2024 onward) as new system leaders rise partly on the basis of at least two decades of failure to improve using an old, ineffective accountability model (test and punish). Put another way, policymakers are beginning to be intrigued. The fact is that top-down assessment does not and cannot work and there are better alternatives that the late Richard Elmore identified in 2014, namely that mutual accountability between the top and other levels working together will get results. Effective accountability trades on explicitness, specificity, transparency, trust, and nonjudgmentalism—all of which occur more naturally when people are participating with a system orientation.

The problem with the top is that they glom onto the "what" (higher test scores, school attendance, and the like) without any notion of the "why" and the "how." You don't build a house by starting with the roof. We start here by having a bottom-up vision *while having the whole system in mind*.

THE SYSTEMNESS MODEL

Fullan (2023a) has already developed part of this model in his book *The Principal 2.0*. His conclusion was that the main role of the principal is to develop the internal or local system (school and community). Coherence and energy must be established at the base level. We also know that the best schools are ones where teachers learn from each other. In these schools, we have learned that teachers must be recognized and valued. We need to figure out how they best learn from each other and how they are sharing, and after a while, this is where we find the best expertise. The best systems (for example, Ottawa and Anaheim) have figured out how to do this in partnership between the district and the schools, and among the schools. We need to figure out what teachers are saying without any fettering. When teachers are working together there is a great deal of accountability built in. There can be a good deal of interaction between the system and the schools, but it is not *trust and verify*; it is *trust and interact*!

If Ottawa Catholic and Anaheim Union High School District can do it, why can't more districts do it? Why can't states create such systems between and among the center, middle, and bottom? You might say that the state will lose control. Guess what? They don't have any control now.

We are stuck in the old paradigm, so there needs to be some new framing of this at the system level—developed jointly by the state and the teachers, students, parents/ community, and school leaders. Call it new policy. As with most of our solutions, they are a set: interaction and synergy with a small number (about seven or eight) of key factors— the simplexity solution. Here is a starter list. They must be done in combination:

1. Increase teacher salaries. Money is never an intrinsic motivator but can be an extrinsic demotivator. The lesson: Make salaries high enough that money is off the table as a major concern.

2. Academic excellence as a stand-alone goal is not an intrinsic motivator. Well-Being and Learning is. Make

it the priority as part of whole child development as the major mission of schools endorsed by teachers' unions (or associations if no union exists). The quid pro quo with teachers is we will pay you well and improve teacher conditions (see other items below) if you commit unequivocally to whole child development (in effect, commit to the humanity paradigm) with teachers, individually and collectively playing a leading role in shaping the solutions.

3. Develop systems, structures, and administrative support at each site to ensure that teachers can cocreate and support peers in whole child development. Have two caring adults for students in the early years. Include master schedules and release time for teachers to work together. Establish showcases to share student work with parents and community. Make school principals part of the development of this local system.

4. Invest in technology integrated with pedagogy to free up time for teachers for enhancing Well-Being and Learning, including student assessment that is transparent and focused on progress with asset-driven versus deficit-driven models about students and families.

5. Develop strong partnerships with the community, including parents, postsecondary institutions, nonprofits, and businesses. Address early learning support, including pathways to careers and community involvement. Every interaction with the local community builds and banks social capital; the process is healing over time.

6. Redefine the teaching profession based on #1–#5 above. Launch a campaign for new teachers based on the new conception. Create roles as teaching assistants, community developers, or apprentices that generate more diversity in the profession, and more candidates seeking what will be a new profession. A crucial point: It is not just new teachers we need, which assumes existing teachers are the problem. Learn from those teachers *who have stayed*! They are a goldmine of what should be done differently. We are talking about

transforming the structure and culture of the teaching profession with newcomers and incumbents who are as close to first responders as you can get. Think social intelligence and make it happen on scale.

7. Reduce to a minimum compliance rules that clog the bureaucracy.

8. Revamp outcome measures so that they reflect a balance of the new measures of progress that balance and integrate academic and Global Competencies, along with well-being measures.

9. Finally, if you want transformation, don't focus on goals that garner little intrinsic motivation (such as becoming more globally competitive). If transformation is the goal, base policies on partnership, not compliance. Be specific, then make it happen together.

So, if you are at the top, and you like the above model, don't just be intrigued—*do something.*

One more piece of advice: Many state and district strategic plans contain a mixture of good ideas and bad ideas that are at least distractors and at most keep us shackled to the status quo. Ask teachers, students, and parents to help sort this out, then delete the detritus. Recall our discussion in Chapter 3 about the amount of potential social intelligence that is being squandered because of the stultified nature of school cultures. Making the changes we recommend would increase social intelligence quantumly.

Before we get to the two vignettes (both of which exemplify Systemness) we need to apply this thinking about Systemness to the most difficult problem of them all—reducing inequity and increasing equality by desiloing them and moving them into the mainstream of system change.

DESILOING INEQUITY AND INEQUALITY

It is getting to the point, because of the impact of the negative part of Driver 3 (increased inequality) that more and more people are ensnared in the inequality syndrome. We need to make it normal to promote Well-Being and Learning wherever it is needed—a need that has increased after decades of inequality magnified by the pandemic. To do this, we have to dig deep into our new knowledge of contextual literacy and of microchange (i.e., change as close to the source of the problem as possible).

Jeff Duncan-Andrade (2022) reminds us that effective systems change is not driven by outcome data. Rather, "meaningful institutional learning is the result of deep investments in process data that examines the processes and practices that produced the outcomes" (p. 19). And then "a commitment to innovate . . . and learn at a much more rapid pace, and in much more collaborative fashion than currently happens in schools" (p. 19).

Duncan-Andrade speaks to the siloing of inequality when he says that we are designing interventions "without any real proximity to the pain they are trying to resolve" (p. 29). The latter is more than being close to the problem. In addition to being close to the problem, what is needed is contextual literacy—"listening closely to solutions born out of the wisdom that comes from living through those experiences." As we found in *Nuance* "empathy for context is an essential requirement for making change with people who live the context every day" (Fullan, 2019, p. 114). Thus, one of our newest change findings is that we need solutions that represent specificity without imposition or, if you prefer, precision without prescription. Without specificity or precision, the solutions are too vague. All of our vignettes involve situations where local or middle level groups are seeking specific solutions cultivating participation and joint problem solving.

The solutions have to arise from detailed understanding of the conditions under which progress has stalled or failed to happen. Among other matters, we know that many of those in poverty are experiencing prolonged "socially toxic environments." Thus, interventions must be based on identifying and understanding the social indicators of health and well-being *specific* to the situation in which they occur.

When we talk about specificity without imposition, we mean that someone has gone to the trouble of understanding the particular context (situation), and has spent corresponding time on purpose, belongingness (relationships), relevance, and responsibility. Duncan-Andrade's (2022) list is the same as ours—his point is that they must be worked through in a context-specific manner where those in poverty are participants in finding new solutions. This is new work, and thus we don't have many examples yet, but the AISNSW example at the end of this chapter contains elements of Systemness, as does San Diego County (Chapter 4) which addresses poverty, and Anaheim (Chapter 3) as they develop new assessment measures that would be of value to other districts and to the overall system itself.

What we are seeing in these developments is the spread of involvement in system change—more precisely, making other people's problems a matter of collective concern. The development of youth includes personal growth, but it also entails connecting to a purpose and identity bigger than ourselves. As Duncan-Andrade (2022) captures it, "A young person cannot be well if they are thriving in school and life while others around them are suffering" (p. 123). Of course, students can sail along despite the problems of peers, but the more that well-being becomes an issue, the more that it affects the whole group.

What we are seeing in these developments is the spread of involvement in system change—more precisely, making other people's problems a matter of collective concern.

Forging greater Systemness is everyone's agenda and is expressed by treating every student and teacher as members of the "system." We marginalize equity if we treat all students the same, or if we treat some differently but fail to get inside their particular circumstance. Anaheim, for example, helps all students find and develop new pathways to further learning and careers. The more we do the latter and share with colleagues in so doing, the more we make equity and equality the core purpose of our work. As such, Systemness for all and by all gets promoted. Anaheim's motto "Unlimited You" is both universal and specific to every individual.

The top still has its job to do. Promote Systemness across the levels. Interact with the middle and bottom on that basis. Invest in and examine progress together with other levels, including new metrics for assessing outcomes (based, for example, on the 6Cs), and talk about how the three levels together, equally, represent the system as a whole. And, if you are fortunate enough to be in a district like Ottawa Catholic as we saw in Chapter 2, the speed of Systemness can be greatly enabled by the top, but note that they also cultivated an enormous amount of bottom-up change that drove Systemness deeper and further.

The top still has its job to do. Promote Systemness across the levels. Interact with the middle and bottom on that basis. Invest in and examine progress together with other levels, including new metrics for assessing outcomes.

In sum, Systemness is defined as the sense that people at all levels of the system are indeed *the system*. If we think simply of three levels—local (school and community), middle (district or regional), and central (state or federal)—we need to consider that all three levels constitute the system. We will revisit this tripartite dynamic of system change in the conclusion of this chapter.

ACTION GUIDELINES FOR SYSTEMNESS

- Select one of the five vignettes (from Chapters 2, 3, 4, and the two vignettes in this chapter) that seems most similar to your own setting and situation. Read it alone or with a group and identify in which ways the vignette represents and fosters Systemness.

- Try as a thought process the reverse engineering we suggested in the previous section: build the base, mobilize the middle, and intrigue the top. Use your own situation to imagine how this might apply to what you could do. Apply the thinking implied in Figure 5.1 to your own situation.

- Take stock of the current place in the system that you and your peers occupy. Consider what leverage you could have in mobilizing positive change from your vantage point.

- Engage in a specific system change endeavor with as much scope as you can find or generate.

We now turn to two additional vignettes. The first is the Association of Independent Schools of New South Wales, which went from a set of loosely coupled individualistic schools to finding their Systemness in a communal effort of school success. Australian school systems consist of three strands, all of which receive school funding—government or state schools, Catholic schools, or independent schools. We are working with all three strands in Australia, but this case is about the independent schools of one of the Australian states, New South Wales. The second case concerns a whole country—Uruguay, South America—that did respect its three levels equally and became a big success because of this.

Driver 4 Vignette 1

Association of Independent Schools of New South Wales

The Association of Independent Schools of New South Wales (AISNSW) began working with us as part of the global Deep Learning partnership in 2018. In fewer than five years they have shifted from a small cluster of innovative schools to a vibrant ecosystem. These schools choose to connect around Deep Learning and are forging new pathways in the design and assessment of learning. We interviewed the leaders of Deep Learning at AISNSW, Jorga Marrum and Chris Morris, to capture the key elements of their journey to greater Systemness.

The AISNSW is in Sydney, Australia. While independent schools make a choice to join the association, 97% of all New South Wales (NSW) independent schools are members. The Sydney-based office supports the 480+ member schools and subcampuses that pay membership fees based on student enrollment. The association is also a peak body, representing an entire sector and advocating for all independent schools in NSW and federally, as the sector enrolls more than 200,000 students. The schools are spread across the Sydney metropolitan area, an urban sprawl from Bondi Beach to the Blue Mountains some eighty kilometers (fifty miles) away, and throughout NSW's vast rural and remote regions where towns and their schools are 100s of kilometers apart.

The NSW Education Standards Authority regulates NSW inde-pendent schools' standards and compliance. The schools are not-for-profit organizations, with rare exceptions, and are inde-pendently governed by a volunteer-based school board or coun-cil. This is where their similarity ends. Independent schools in NSW could not be further from being a cohesive school system or geographical school district. What characterizes member schools is their diversity. Unlike other sectors, most independent schools operate autonomously and are separately accountable to their parent and school communities. Parents send their children to NSW independent schools because of this diversity, the right to choose education delivery, and the communities they attract. As a result, the group is the fastest-growing school sector in NSW.

The diversity comes from each school's autonomy. Schools choose their educational ethos, philosophy, or focus; nominate a religious affiliation or none; and employ the teaching and nonteaching staff they prefer. Importantly, they control their own budgets, derived from a combined revenue of the tuition fees, ranging from $2,000 per year to more than $40,000 per child, and tiered government funding.

Getting Started

While they are disparate schools, independent schools in NSW align in their demand for high-quality professional learning for their teachers, particularly around innovation. As a result, AISNSW education consultants annually design and deliver more than 300 tailored face-to-face, blended, and online courses, conferences, and programs across educational leadership, research, and practice.

AISNSW joined the New Pedagogies for Deep Learning global partnership in 2018 because of the evidence and a reputation for enhancing teachers' classroom practices to develop students' general capabilities. AISNSW already encouraged schools to utilize consultants' expertise to codesign and deliver professional learning tailored to their school. So much about the global partnership aligned with AISNSW established consultancy model. However, the global partnership's potential for longer-term consultancy over months and even years was even more attractive.

An open invitation launch event to all member and nonmember independent schools was sent in July 2018, after which they could express interest in joining the Deep Learning Network in its first year.

The Journey

The AISNSW Designing for Deep Learning Network One started in September 2018 with fourteen schools under a three-year agreement. As expected, some schools had low-fee structures and small to medium size enrollments of between forty and 350 students. Some were from rural and regional areas of NSW, and others were large multicampus colleges in metropolitan Sydney with more than 1,000 students and billing parents with significant tuition fees. The cultural diversity of faiths, philosophies, and ethos was present. The challenge was in building a unified network. How would such a diverse range of schools, with little commonality, create a collective focus?

To enable connection and sharing across the schools, AISNSW committed two full-time leaders to support the Deep Learning Network, initially to learn the work and then to support schools in the field. In October 2018, the fourteen schools also came together for their first network event, a two-day capacity-building forum run by the New Pedagogies for Deep Learning global team.

That day teachers met the dedicated AISNSW Deep Learning consultant assigned to them for the three-year agreement.

Next, the principal and senior leaders selected a Core Team, a small group of appropriate leaders and enthusiastic teachers. They initially learned the work, crafted vision and goals, and designed an implementation plan based on needs and promising practices. These lead-learners advocated strongly for the work and led by doing. The Team Lead was designated from within the Core Team and was a critical communication conduit between the school and the AISNSW consultant. It was important that they saw themselves as the driver of the work in the school and utilized the eight in-school visits from their consultant throughout the year.

The AISNSW consultant supported each of their allocated schools with a range of professional learning, including

- Core team workshops to establish, for example, school vision and goals, or to assess school conditions
- Core team project planning over the timeline of consultancy
- Facilitated workshops with groups of teachers and the whole staff
- Collaborative design sessions with teams of teachers

A dedicated consultant was and still is critical to the Deep Learning engagement for AISNSW. Each AISNSW consultant has an instructional, educational leadership background, with a sound knowledge of the NSW-mandated curriculum from kindergarten to Year 12. Building relational trust with the different schools' Core Teams and Team Lead is equally essential. The familiar consultant quickly fits in and learns to be responsive within each school's context while making sure their role is gradually made redundant. The focus is on creating sustainable conditions for Deep Learning to become "the way we do things around here."

Additionally, an external voice better ensures momentum in enacting change. The role of the consultant is as an expert in the work, collaborator, and coach rather than a driver of implementation. Successful schools demonstrate open communication, frequently checking their thinking for implementation with their consultant.

Each July's annual launch invitation and expression of interest has engaged forty-one schools in Deep Learning over five years. Over the years, the processes and protocols consultants use with in-school Core Teams in the first six to nine months have increased in fidelity. The consultants now have evidence of what works well to excite, motivate, and inspire Core Teams. What works is:

- **Get the right lead-learners early.** Establishing norms and clarity around the roles of the Team Lead and Core Team members is crucial. If the right people are involved early and committed to implementing and testing the work, they will become optimistic advocates with influence.

- **Develop a coherent and compelling case for change.** The school's narrative should acknowledge what has come before and why Deep Learning is the right direction for now. Imperatives help the Core Team and senior executive to have a consistent and compelling answer to any curly questions. The new narrative needs to instill trust and hope rather than be just another change initiative that will come and go.

- **Learn the work and the power of the tools.** New Pedagogies for Deep Learning is not a tasting menu. There is necessary complexity in sequencing the pathways to the six competencies and the learning progressions to provide measurable progress. Yet, despite the rigor, teachers are excited when they see how the work can begin to live within their school and when they identify the promising practices that may become the connection points.

- **Develop a personalized implementation plan.** It is imperative to conduct the School Conditions Assessment because of its power to support school executives in understanding the conditions needed if people are to lean into change voluntarily. First and foremost, the change schools are preparing for is mindset and culture.

- **Leverage digital to ensure momentum.** Consultants must remain relevant when they are not in the school. For example, schools add the consultant to their virtual learning environments to maintain connection.

The Network to Systemness

In explaining the autonomy in decision-making for independent schools as different from government-run or Catholic systemic schools in NSW, there is a resultant effect to highlight. Sharing ideas and practices across independent schools is not the norm. Further, independent schools provide families with a choice of diverse philosophies, ethos, religious affiliations, and other differentiators. As a result, the schools are in a marketplace as competitors for enrollment. The business model where schools compete for students does not make a Deep Learning Network a comfortable environment for Systemness to emerge. It is noteworthy that in this case, the benefits of collaborative learning outweighed the natural tendency to compete.

Despite this, and ironically because of it, the Deep Learning Network is attractive for independent school teachers because it affords them opportunities to exchange experience and practice that they wouldn't otherwise have. Going "outside" to learn "inside" is a crucial lever for change, and AISNSW consultants have reinforced the value of this over other detractors to ensure there are opportunities for more teachers to be involved.

For example, AISNSW consultants began Team Lead online webinars in the first year. They were formal, preplanned, and instructional without opportunity for sharing. Attendance dropped off quickly. As schools got into the work, the consultants in the field observed great implementation ideas and knew this was worth sharing. So, the webinars' purpose shifted to ideas, insights, approaches, and assets. As the months progressed, the AISNSW consultants heard stories of success from schools. The informal exchange of stories nudged and inspired others to try different things. It was evident the Deep Learning Network could continue to grow with consultants on the ground in every school, documenting and sharing stories of success and creating a future repository.

The change also meant Deep Learning stories surfaced quickly. Teachers were designing and loving it, energized by sharing evidence of impact. It wasn't seen as more work but legitimized and validated their effort. There was a sense of pride when teachers shared with others.

An important Deep Learning Network role for the AISNSW consultant is to record as many stories as possible in print, video, or teacher presentation and store them in what is called a Vignette Vault. With more than fifty examples of Deep Learning in action, including evidence of impact, the vault is a valuable resource for the Deep Learning Network to access. In addition, teachers often request examples of Deep Learning in their subject area and for different year groups.

Teachers present these stories face-to-face or online at the Deep Learning Network level and at professional learning events. Creating opportunities for design teams to share stories of success with colleagues in their school, and at the Deep Learning Network level, changes perceptions—positive experiences validate the work and encourage others.

Fundamental Change in the System

AISNSW sees potential for a fundamental shift toward a systemic change in all NSW schools. Curriculum reform is being implemented over the next five years by the NSW Education Standards Authority and is the first significant change in thirty years. Declining teacher trainees and increasing resignations from the profession, combined with student disengagement, have also added to an imperative for change that is acknowledged from the top down. Change must happen.

Educators in independent schools where Deep Learning is the focus are shifting away from models that inhibit teachers' innovation capacity. Instead, they question what is essential and of value for student learning, particularly in secondary education. Moreover, they can do this with autonomy.

At the local Deep Learning Network level, independent school teachers and executive educators observe and hear reports of increased student engagement and read the evidence of improved academic performance. They connect this change in students' learning behaviors with the attention given to enhancing competencies through explicit and intentional teaching.

AISNSW consultants also see at the Deep Learning Network level that teachers enjoying teaching—at a time when reportedly morale is bottomed out and the profession is declining. Deep Learning teachers report how satisfying it is to see their students enjoy and engage in the learning they have designed for them. They want more time in the collaborative design process with colleagues to deepen every learning experience. Students and their teachers are the fundamental activists in education, and they are rallying now in the Deep Learning space to create momentum for system change.

The AISNSW experience highlights the complexity of external support systems but also what is possible without direct line authority. So, how is AISNSW able to create a coherent direction across diverse schools when many intact districts and municipalities do not? Some of the factors at play we noted are:

- **Joint Determination.** Schools are choosing to become a network because it helps them reach their unique goals. The structure of support through the Core Lead team at the school ensures that all decisions are tailored to local needs yet provides them the external expertise.

- **Contextual Literacy.** The AISNSW consultants have a deep understanding of both the local contexts and the wider governmental trends and requirements. They can provide customized support while also drawing on their global and national connections.

- **External Catalyst.** This cluster is demonstrating our philosophy of "Go Outside to Get Better Inside" at multiple levels. The schools are connected to the AISNSW consultants and each other but also to other schools in a global network spanning twenty countries. A second layer of connection occurs at the leadership level, where the AISNSW consultants are connected to a strong global network of leaders. They are accessing and sharing the latest research, trends, and strategies across the globe. This feeds fresh ideas into the mix while validating and showcasing the impact.

- **Learn From the Work.** Organizations that are growing expertise and innovating have strong mechanisms to learn from experience. This cluster uses a variety of approaches to build lateral capacity (interschool) and intraschool capacity. A range of capacity-building approaches—webinars, workshops, showcases, and visitations—develop common language, expertise, and shared understanding. A repository of exemplars, videos, and vignettes recognizes and celebrates progress while creating a pathway to engage more deeply. AISNSW recently sponsored a Regional Asia Pacific Deep Learning Lab to showcase the results and progress of current schools while attracting new schools to join. These sustained cycles of celebration combined with intentional infusion of new ideas are amplifying efforts and engagement.

- **System Orientation.** We noted earlier the need to build the base and mobilize the middle. In this example, we see that liberating the teachers and building their capacity, energy, and expertise is mobilizing the middle to come together as schools despite the competitive environment. As teachers shift their practices, students become ambassadors for the new way of learning, school leaders are influenced to devote even more resources, parents are impressed, and the whole system mindset emerges.

AISNSW is a telling example because independent schools have a tendency to prize their independence, and in many ways, the fallback position is to go your own way. What forces could pry them from this cherished autonomy to embracing a full-on communal endeavor? Could it be that the Systemness of their effort is the big attractor? More and more, we think that schools will be attracted to the proposition of working in clusters to pursue and achieve deeper purposes.

How about an example of a much larger proposition? The transformation of a whole country!

Driver 4 Vignette 2

Uruguay

Uruguay is a small country on the southeast coast of South America with a population of 3.5 million people. It has a high rate of literacy and is a safe country with a strong commitment to democracy. Its constitution allows the president only one four-year term (and a second term if there is a four-year gap), recognizing that political stability is dependent on democracy. In 2007, Uruguay established a new separate entity at the national level called Plan Ceibal, intended to be a short-term innovation (hence the designation "plan"). Incidentally and revealingly, the Uruguay government passed legislation in 2023 to drop the word "Plan," and to retain the official designation as "Ceibal." This is a remarkable step because it makes the innovative agency Ceibal an official and permanent part of the government.

In the beginning, Ceibal's purpose was to oversee the establishment of one laptop per student at the primary level to introduce computers as a gateway to knowledge and innovation to all students in primary schools (Grades 1–6). On October 13, 2009, a new computer, called the XO model, was distributed to all students. It cost the government $260 per pupil. Plan Ceibal's mandate was to oversee the development of technology and new knowledge for all primary students in the country.

In 2010, the president of Ceibal, Miguel Brechner, invited Michael Fullan to assess the potential of the XO for transforming knowledge and learning in the country. Fullan's main recommendation was that computers would make little difference unless they were linked to the related development of pedagogy and learning for all teachers and students in the country. Therein began the strategy that Plan Ceibal developed *jointly with the system*, resulting in such remarkable success that the government recently celebrated in its fifteenth anniversary of Ceibal (established in 2007). It was at this time that the government dropped the word "Plan" and signaled that Ceibal was now a permanent government agency.

We don't think that Ceibal had a grand plan of implementation, but its leadership seemed to have all the right instincts along the way, which we try to capture in this brief vignette. Plan Ceibal was one of the founding members of New Pedagogies for Deep Learning (NPDL) beginning in 2014, with 100 schools (adding others as they proceeded to the current total of more than 700 schools, which is 50% of the total). In this vignette, we can only highlight the elements that enabled whole system success. Most of these factors were parallel in that they interacted to multiply impact. Six interacting elements stand out to us:

1. Initially, Ceibal was a new innovation unit that had a degree of independence with its own president. Parallel to it was the National Public Education Administration (ANEP) and the Ministry of Education overseeing schools with a large group of inspectors—the basic bureaucratic system, if you will. The leadership of Ceibal, and of ANEP, made it a point to build relationships, share ideas, and jointly celebrate success. Anytime we were in Montevideo (the capital of Uruguay) we participated in the interaction across these entities. We interviewed inspectors as well as Ceibal staff. When the high-profile, high-attendance tenth anniversary of Ceibal was held in 2017, the minister of education and the president of Ceibal were front and center celebrating the event. Rarely does one witness such cohesion and camaraderie across semi-independent entities.

2. Simultaneously, Ceibal developed innovative initiatives with local schools and communities. It turns out that teachers and especially students had a taste for technology and innovation (robotics, local projects to redirect rainwater into use for gardens and vegetables, etc.; see our Uruguay video file at https://deep-learning.global). This was an illustration of what we call the "start slow, go fast" phenomenon. We heard stories where at first the computers stayed in their boxes until eventually, curious students asked their teachers if they could open them. This led to a lot of experimentation. Once Ceibal started to initiate innovation there were many willing participants, which rapidly led to an impressive number of projects. This liberated many teachers from traditional teaching—a point that we come back to shortly.

3. Ceibal and its schools participate actively in external learning with other members of the Global Deep Learning Partnership. NPDL members participated in monthly cluster calls, regional meetings (Asia and North and South America), and a once-a-year Deep Dive in-person (except for the COVID hiatus). Uruguay is a very active member in all of these (we have simultaneous translation, and all key material is available in Spanish).

4. Uruguay has been able to manage the centralization-decentralization dilemma. Policies are less imposed and more invitational, leveraging peers, case examples of success, and regular celebrations. Capacity building is strong and intentional across all levels of the systems so that there is widespread understanding of the reform and people's role in supporting it. Sharing of the best ideas is widely practiced.

5. Policy innovation has become part and parcel of the evolution. For example, the new plan of ANEP (the official curriculum) defines ten competencies in two domains:

Domain 1

- Communication

- Creative thinking

- Critical thinking

- Scientific thinking

- Computational thinking

- Metacognitive competence

Domain 2

- Intrapersonal

- Initiative and orientation to action

- Interpersonal relations (with others)

- Local, global, and digital citizenship

Recently, there was a new release of a policy document containing the new progressions of competencies. All of these are compatible with new policies to move away from standard tests to Global Competencies.

6. Last, it is likely that Ceibal will establish two branches: one to continue its intracountry development and the other as an entity to help support other South American countries to develop in these same directions (such as Argentina, Paraguay, Brazil, Chile)—something that it is already doing on a small scale.

Ceibal has had two presidents with whom we have and are working: Miguel Brechner (founding president) and Leandro Folgar (president since 2020). We interviewed each of them. We asked Folgar to share the main ideas that Ceibal is most proud of. Here is his response:

1. The fact that Ceibal has become a state policy that has evolved over the course of four governments—two of them formed by different political parties.

2. Ceibal is now a permanent agency (Government Innovation Agency), no longer a temporary Plan Ceibal.

3. The vision of forming a high-performance team with talent from multidisciplinary areas at the service of equity, inclusion, and education.

4. The way Ceibal contributed to bridging the digital divide in the country, making devices and internet connection equally accessible for our students.

5. How Ceibal offered a way to mitigate the tremendously negative effects of the pandemic in education. And how it was recognized by the international community. Always prioritizing equity, inclusion, and innovation.

6. The fact that Ceibal is successful not because it was one of the first implementations of One Laptop Per Child (OLPC) in South America but because it reinvented the OLPC concept to fit Uruguayans' needs and sustained the efforts even after the first successes to make Ceibal grow every step of the way.

7. The way Ceibal permanently strives to learn from the future in order to make technology, innovation, and quality education equally accessible at a national scale. (personal interview, 2022)

We were also interested in asking the founding president, Brechner, what Uruguayan students were like prior to Plan Ceibal. The readers will see in the video vignettes that the students are incredibly open and enthusiastic. They are curious and innovative with their peers, with teachers, and with peers across schools. They readily take up new ideas, robotics, community projects, and so on. Their behavior is genuine and it's a marvel! So, our question to President Brechner was: Prior to NPDL, were Uruguayan students always this enthusiastic? Here is his response:

> Mostly they were sitting at desks in rows, listening to teachers. NPDL and Ceibal have very much changed this. They have allowed many liberties in the way teaching is done. The more advanced schools have taken the opportunity to do things differently. For me, there is no doubt that many things have changed. The more that schools do different things, the easier it is to build momentum for rebuilding the education system. (personal interview, 2022)

In summary, Uruguay has accomplished what few other systems have been able to do, such as

1. Spread technology universally throughout the country in the service of learning.
2. Involve the schools in determining the nature of innovations and their use—what we call jointly determining innovation.
3. Establish rapport with local towns and communities throughout the country.
4. Develop and maintain support and a shared sense of ownership with the ANEP.
5. Maintain the political support of the president and political sectors.
6. Become a permanent member of the government structure.

It is also no accident that Uruguay's response to COVID has been stronger than other countries in South America. Rieble-Aubourg and Viteri (2020) found that Uruguay is the only country in the region that had basic digital conditions to support learning (connectivity, digital platforms, virtual tutoring, digital resources packages, and a central digital warehouse); by contrast, in other countries only 36% of schools have "suitable software and computing power" (cited in Fullan & Quinn, 2020). Uruguay's investment in capacity building focused on Deep Learning and system changes at all levels continued during the COVID-19 pandemic. As COVID-19 hit, the Core Deep Learning Team was able to **leverage the strong communication links and digital infrastructure** already established with teachers, to continue communicating, teaching, and learning with agility.

Low bandwidth was combated by using phones and WhatsApp. **Television was activated as a daily medium to continue to connect, teach, and learn.** The notion of "Momentos de Aprendizaje Profundo" (Deep Learning Moments) was established to stay true to the principles of Deep Learning while easing the pressure on teachers to think in terms of smaller innovations. They posed the question, "In all we do in our teaching, however large or small, how do we continue to plan and generate those small opportunities for Deep Learning to occur?"

Thus, we have whole system success. We don't expect many countries to have the conditions and wherewithal to pull off a fifteen-year-run building such a thorough system of success. So, we refer the reader back to our discussion of Systemness and the importance of the bottom and middle to success. In Uruguay, the bottom and middle were a large part of its success. An innovative entity—Ceibal, with no formal hierarchical authority—and a strong Systemness orientation built a powerful system where all parts of the country helped develop the solution.

COHERENCE MAKING

In terms of system change per se, the fact is that we are in turmoil and confusion after decades of decline, and the radical disruption of the pandemic. System change is in the air, and the question is which way will it go—for the worse or for the better? Yes, we are optimists, but we also believe that there is reason for hope. Many will know of the Irish poet William Yeats's dramatic poem in 1920, called *The Second Coming*. Part of it reads:

> Things fall apart, the center cannot hold,
> Mere Anarchy is loosed upon the world.

It turned out that Yeats was right in being pessimistic; there followed the Great Depression and World War II, more than twenty-five years of misery. Things are different now. Complexity is less predictable, and deep problems are on the rise. Here is our take. When the system begins to obviously fail, individuals and groups in democracies begin to act out. There is a palpable growing sense of negativism. Then sooner than later (and this is admittedly speculative) other individuals begin to openly act nicer and kinder. Such individuals become more obvious (including to each other). They are, in a word, more attracted to the action that the drivers thinking provides. They become attracted to and committed to collective action. They are found, for example, in the five vignettes in this book. Positive change ensues at an active pace—*even when the "system" is not actively supporting it!* The message to system leaders seems clear to us. Help develop the middle and lower "systems" and join forces to help cause greater overall system transformation. Our Systemness Model outlined above is a direct invitation to all three levels to develop and make this new model work.

The message to system leaders seems clear to us. Help develop the middle and lower "systems" and join forces to help cause greater overall system transformation.

In sum, in the past four chapters we have completed our account of the four drivers along with five vignettes of selected drivers in action. We have referred to the growing role of our model of Deep Learning as it provides some of the depth of action required to bring about substantial system transformation. No matter how you cut it, the four drivers are deep into affecting practice and outcomes. For each driver, the experience of explicitly using the driver, individually and collectively, is an exercise in meaning making. People learn what it means to use the driver and to create and assess the causal link to outcomes. Participants and leaders talk about it, demonstrate it, make videos about it, cross-visit to see it in action, and process what they know in order to refine their own practices. They relate all of this to policy contexts, although we have argued that the latter (policies) are not clearly developed. Good systems, such as those reflected by our five vignettes, ultimately make their own judgments, but they reach out horizontally to contribute to and learn from peers, and vertically to try to influence, be informed by policies, and be helped by available system resources. If you want to have any chance of transformation, *you have to help the whole system learn.*

Finally, the drivers align very well with our Deep Learning Framework. Our vignettes show how some sites (Ottawa and Uruguay) incorporated Deep Learning early on whereas other sites (Anaheim, San Diego County, and AISNSW) turned to Deep Learning to further their work. The four drivers and Deep Learning fit well with each other. It is time then to examine the Deep Learning Framework directly.

. . . .

CHAPTER 6

Deep Learning
The Future Depends on It

O ur **Deep Learning** solution can transform learning in a way that develops the capacity of humans, individually and collectively, to cope and thrive in an ever-complex, dangerous, and potentially magnificent civilization.

---

*Our **Deep Learning** solution can transform learning in a way that develops the capacity of humans, individually and collectively, to cope and thrive in an ever-complex, dangerous, and potentially magnificent civilization.*

The **Deep Learning Approach, as we have developed it**, is not to be confused with the term *deep learning*, which was coined by scientists in the past century as they began to experiment with computer models based on neural networks. A quick online search will produce a definition of deep learning as part of a family of machine-learning methods. The latest sophisticated addition to the machine intelligence family is ChatGPT (OpenAI, 2022), which is an artificial language model that can generate realistic human-like text, such as producing a cogent essay on any topic in seconds. Other AI competitors have now joined the race. Who will serve you? ChatGPT, Bard (Google), Claude (Anthropic), Ernie (Baidu), etc.? Artificial intelligence has been developing at a faster rate than its counterpart human or social intelligence in recent years. Our drivers' framework aims to mobilize the humanity paradigm in relation to AI (see also Broussard, 2023; Lobel, 2022). We will focus in this chapter on a comprehensive solution—**Deep Learning (DL)**, which is a vehicle to integrate the four drivers into an accessible framework as a catalyst for the humanity paradigm.

THE DEEP LEARNING APPROACH

The world of education has been upended by the intertwined challenges posed by the pandemic, growing inequality, poverty, climate deterioration, and the reduction of trust across the globe. The sense of being overwhelmed is palpable and trying to patch up the status quo is no longer viable. If we want learners who can thrive in turbulent times, solve complex problems, and change their world, then we must reimagine learning and unleash a powerful model for transformation.

When the status quo no longer works, an alternative is needed. The exciting finding is that an increasing number of schools and systems, including students, teachers, leaders, and communities are strongly attracted to what we call Deep Learning. This interest has accelerated since the pandemic began in early 2020. There is a growing recognition worldwide that a transformative change is needed and that the comprehensive Deep Learning Framework is offering a way to mobilize all levels of the system simultaneously.

We have been working with clusters of schools, communities, and governments since 2014 and are seeing the integrated approach gain traction. What is most promising is that the combination of integrated factors in the Deep Learning Framework is powerful within regional and local contexts, and equally impactful across diverse contexts in more than twenty countries. The examples in this book and on our website (https://deep-learning.global) represent the early adopters; it is noteworthy that we are also experiencing a recent surge of interest in Deep Learning.

At the same time, there is a growing global recognition that it is time for a seismic shift. Andreas Schleicher, director of the Organisation for Economic Co-operation and Development, stated:

> Education is no longer just about teaching students something, it's about helping each and every one of our students to develop a reliable compass and tools to navigate with confidence through an increasingly complex, volatile, and uncertain world. Success in education is about building curiosity—opening minds; it is about compassion—opening hearts; and it is about courage—mobilizing our cognitive, social, and emotional resources to take action. (2021)

Jobs and life in the future will require foundational skills, of course, but also key competencies that cannot be taught by artificial intelligence like creativity and collaboration, plus vital human character qualities like compassion, curiosity, resilience, and adaptability. Our Deep Learning Framework is fundamentally different from traditional schooling. As you will see, it transforms the purpose of learning; the competencies; the essence of pedagogy, particularly the relationships and culture of learning; the conditions that foster learning; and above all, the outcomes. Together, this approach helps individuals, groups, and society to cope with existing problems and create a better future.

The Deep Learning Framework creates a common language through comprehensive tools and processes and galvanizes a shared understanding that builds coherence, collective purpose, and professionalism within schools, networks, and whole jurisdictions. It represents a radical new purpose for schooling, for simultaneously learning about and creating a new future.

BELIEFS IN ACTION

This bold undertaking has critical foundations in shared beliefs and values that guide the way we interact with each other and with students and families. Take a moment to read the eight belief statements in Figure 6.1 and reflect on the statements that most resonate for you and your context.

FIGURE 6.1 ● Deep Learning Beliefs and Values

We Believe

Education is the most powerful force for improving the world by transforming individuals and systems.

The **Global Competencies** unlesh the potential of **ALL** learners to **flourish** in learning and life. Deep Learning is the process of developing the Global Competencies.

Equity, Well-Being, and Deep Learning have synergy; they are dynamically integrated and reinforce each other.

Students are Changemakers. When their Voice, Choice, Agency, and Leadership are liberated, they make a difference in the world.

An appreciative, asset-based lens allows everyone to become their best selves.

The **Global Knowledge-Building Partnership** accelerates our collective innovation, impact, and influence.

Collaboration Matters and is informed by relationships, context, co-design, and localized solution finding.

Learning by Doing empowers everyone to experience, reflect, grow, and change.

Source: © Education in Motion, New Pedagogies for Deep Learning™ (NPDL), 2020.

The big challenge for humanity is how to make this shift in the purpose and practice of learning for *all* students in every classroom across the world, regardless of context or circumstance. What differentiates our approach from many others is its focus on the whole child, not the single agenda of academic achievement. As such, the approach explicitly focuses on a whole system solution. It begins with individual students and teachers but always with the intent of diffusing impact to all. It is powerful as an integrated approach because it simultaneously addresses well-being, equity, and learning.

WHAT'S DEEP ABOUT DEEP LEARNING?

Deep Learning is quality learning that sticks for life. It engages and motivates learners to develop the competencies they will need to navigate life now and in the future through real-life experiences that have meaning and purpose and foster higher-level cognitive processes.

Deep Learning is quality learning that sticks for life. It engages and motivates learners to develop the competencies they will need to navigate life now and in the future through real-life experiences that have meaning and purpose and foster higher-level cognitive processes.

Learning moves from traditional to deep across four dimensions:

1. *Purpose* shifts from transmitting existing knowledge to real-world problem solving that creates new knowledge,

2. *Control* shifts from teachers as sole decision makers to students becoming codesigners of the learning in partnership, and

3. *Student voice*, choice, and agency shift from students being compliant, passive learners to taking responsibility as independent inquirers.

4. Students became *active system change agents* working in partnership with each other, teachers, and beyond.

THE DEEP LEARNING FRAMEWORK: SIMPLEXITY IN ACTION

THE NEW PURPOSE OF EDUCATION

The new purpose of education focuses on the development of the individual, the group, and society in concert. It builds capacities for coping and thriving amid the problems and opportunities of dynamically complex societies and fosters a sense of purpose, belonging, and contribution. The Deep Learning Framework provides a pathway to enact this new purpose. The framework for action is a good example of what we call **simplexity** that we introduced in Chapter 5—the smallest number of components needed to address a complex issue. The simple part of the Deep Learning Framework is that there are only three key components. The complex part is integrating the components as an integrated set to achieve the new purpose of schooling (see also Figure 6.2).

In considering the internal essence of the framework, consider it in the context of the purpose and outcomes of the new humanity-based learning we have been examining throughout this book. The new purpose is to foster the development of all students who are equipped individually and collectively to cope with and to help transform a society that is currently deeply flawed. The Deep Learning Framework over time is intended to enable this profound change in our society by providing a pathway to move from the status quo. Part and parcel of our model includes working on new assessments of the 6Cs in practice. In this sense, students will already be immersed in societal change as they hit the ground running for a lifetime of struggle, learning, and impact on the world like no previous generation.

Recall the new core purpose of Well-Being and Learning: *To cultivate civic-minded changemakers who make a difference in their own lives and in society.* The Deep Learning Framework provides a structure for enacting this purpose.

THE DEEP LEARNING FRAMEWORK

1. **Global Competencies:** Six Global Competencies that define the outcomes of Deep Learning

2. **Learning Design:** Four elements of learning design that help teachers craft robust, real-world learning experiences

3. **Learning Conditions:** Three learning condition rubrics that identify the conditions needed in schools, districts, and systems to support Deep Learning

FIGURE 6.2 ● The Deep Learning Framework

New Pedagogies for
Deep Learning
A GLOBAL PARTNERSHIP

© New Pedagogies for
Deep Learning 2023

Source: © Education in Motion, New Pedagogies for Deep Learning™ (NPDL), 2020.

1. GLOBAL COMPETENCIES

The first step in transforming learning at scale was to build a common purpose and goals. Six Global Competencies (6Cs) clarify what is essential to know and be able to do and be like as human citizens. These 6Cs of *character/compassion, citizenship, collaboration, communication, creativity, and critical thinking* unleash the potential of every child. In the original formulation, compassion was seen as a subcomponent of character, but in the new formulation it has been elevated as a co-C with character. Compassion is empathy with action. It has become all the more prominent as the humanity paradigm becomes more pronounced in pandemic times when the plight of humanity has become more poignant. Anaheim has recognized compassion as a prominent C, as has Peter Senge in their new initiative "developing compassionate system leaders" (Senge & Böll, 2023). Character and compassion combine to lead system change.

Each competency is essential for the development of youth, and the adults who work with them. As a set, the Cs are synergistic. Deep Learning is the process of developing these Global Competencies (6Cs) that are needed to flourish in a dynamic world. When immersed in Deep Learning experiences that are relevant and challenging, students learn more, and it sticks—we call this being good at learning and good at life.

The 6Cs have been validated over the past decade as countries have used the common language to build shared understanding with other teachers, students, and parents. The 6Cs are an anchor for conversations about the design of learning as well as ways to measure growth. Each competency has a set of dimensions that provide greater depth and precision (see Figure 6.3).

Learning progressions were created for each competency to describe the pathway for development and the knowledge, skills, and behaviors at each of the five levels of proficiency: limited, emerging, developing, accelerating, and advanced. These tools serve as anchors to help students, teachers, and families design learning and discuss growth.

FIGURE 6.3 ● Defining the Six Global Competencies for Deep Learning

Character/Compassion

- Proactive stance toward life and learning to learn
- Tenacity, perseverance, and resilience
- Empathy, compassion, and integrity in action

Citizenship

- A global perspective
- Commitment to human equity and well-being through empathy and compassion for diverse values and world views
- Genuine interest in human and environmental sustainability
- Solving ambiguous and complex problems in the real world to benefit citizens

Collaboration

- Working interdependently as a team
- Interpersonal and team-related skills
- Social, emotional, and intercultural skills
- Managing team dynamics and challenges

Communication

- Communication designed for audience and impact
- Message advocates a purpose and makes an impact
- Reflection to further develop and improve communication
- Voice and identity expressed to advance humanity

Creativity

- Economic and social entrepreneurialism
- Asking the right inquiry questions
- Pursuing and expressing novel ideas and solutions
- Leadership to turn ideas into action

Critical Thinking

- Evaluating information and arguments
- Making connections and identifying patterns
- Meaningful knowledge construction
- Experimenting, reflecting, and taking action on ideas in the real world

© New Pedagogies for Deep Learning™ 2023

New Pedagogies for
Deep Learning™
A GLOBAL PARTNERSHIP

Source: © Education in Motion, New Pedagogies for Deep Learning™ (NPDL), 2023.

Learning is never static, and the world is constantly evolving. We could never have predicted the Black Lives Matter or #MeToo movements, a global pandemic, or the devastating impacts of poverty and climate change. The truth is that humanity has never faced such a mixture of dynamic complexity.

Over the past three years especially, Deep Learning schools and districts noted that the clarity of the 6C concepts combined with the precision of the dimensions and progressions gave consistency of practice and have fostered a deep professional community of sharing practice. The caution that people had was, don't just go with the surface label; go deep into the meaning of each C using the progressions.

Refinements to the 6Cs reflect emerging world issues. The issues of *equity, equality, and social justice* have much greater urgency and thus have more prominence in the dimensions. New definitions of belongingness and poverty require shifts in mindset. The emerging worldwide focus on *well-being* has prompted further elaboration on what it means to be well. *Compassion* (empathy combined with action) has much-elevated importance in tandem with the character competency. As the new purpose of learning shifts from an individual attainment to contribution to community and society it is essential to be explicit about the quality of compassion we need as humans.

The 6Cs are compelling, accessible, and energizing. Once they are embraced, the real challenge is helping scores of teachers to shift their pedagogical practices. The second component, the Four Elements of Learning Design, accelerates the shift in teacher practice from traditional to new practices by supporting teachers to create Deep Learning experiences based on the cultural history and contexts of students.

2. FOUR ELEMENTS OF LEARNING DESIGN

The four elements of Deep Learning Design are the essence of the transformation through a radical change in *pedagogy*—the way students learn and what they learn. Part and parcel of DL is that caring and learning relationships, *linked to the culture and experiences of students*, form the basis of new learning. This is obviously crucial for Equity-Equality, but it also applies to the "wounded winners" that Michael Sandel (2020) identified (previously successful students who no longer find the academic grind tolerable).

Four elements (see Figure 6.4) work in concert to create the new pedagogies that foster Deep Learning. Each element represents a set of decision points that teachers make to address the unique needs of their learners and contexts. These elements require new student relationships with teachers and others and must be linked to the culture and experiences of students. We'll explore the essential features of each element and the decisions that impact the learning design.

FIGURE 6.4 ● Four Elements of Learning Design

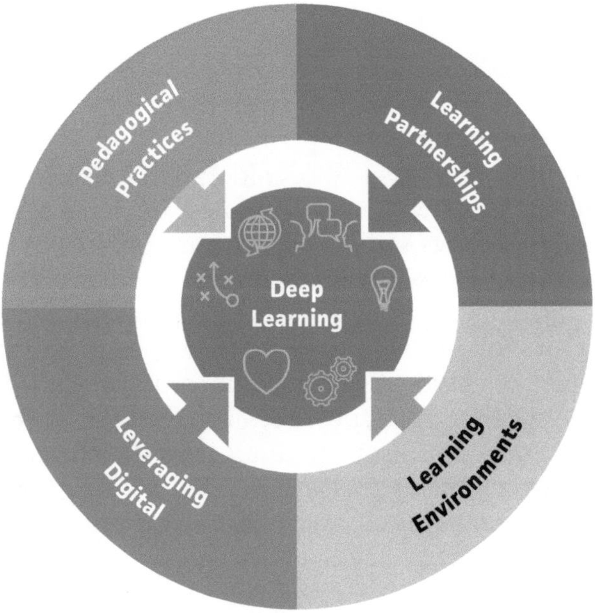

© Education in Motion, New Pedagogies for Deep Learning™ 2023

Source: © Education in Motion, New Pedagogies for Deep Learning™ (NPDL), 2023.

Learning Partnerships focus on the relationships between students and teachers but also with parents, experts, business and community partners, and schools across the globe. These new relationships shift voice, control, and interactions, and open up opportunities to connect to real-world issues. This more authentic learning moves beyond the classroom walls and builds on interests and talents organically. As relationships deepen, student voice amplifies, and they become codesigners and coconstructors of the learning. One way this begins is by teachers increasing authentic choices and providing optional ways for students to demonstrate their learning. As trust develops, students take on more self-monitoring and responsibility for their learning. Teachers need to scaffold the learning so that students have the skills to collaborate, give feedback, and make wise decisions. This new role of students as codesigners increases student engagement and pushes on the traditional role of teachers to find the balance of structure and independence.

Learning Environments has two interrelated aspects: the culture of learning and the physical or virtual environment. Creating cultures of learning that support every child to flourish is more essential than ever. Recognition that we must address the needs of those who have struggled and have been marginalized means we must create learning spaces of belonging that are psychologically safe and foster collaboration and risk-taking. This begins when teachers know their students' context and intentionally create norms of belonging where every voice is heard and respected, empathy and compassion are modeled by deeply listening to student needs and interests, and learning opportunities are structured to help students feel competent as learners. This culture creates high engagement, sense of self, and purpose. Students are craving this opportunity to be heard and valued.

Working in concert with the new *culture of learning* is the *physical or virtual learning environment*. If we want students to be curious, connected collaborators we need to provide multidimensional spaces that offer flexibility for collaboration; quiet places for reflection; active areas for investigation, inquiry, and communication; and rich resources that are transparently accessible. If we want students to seek out experts in the community and beyond and to build knowledge from multiple fields, we need to help them identify ways to connect, skills to discern sources critically, and ways to build relationships in a diverse world.

One positive outcome of the pandemic has been the amplification of connections to teachers and students across the globe who are learning from and with one another. The combination of access to diverse perspectives and cultures combined with a culture of belongingness and safety is fostering a new curriculum of humanity. Learning environments are changing rapidly both culturally as new partnerships emerge and physically as the walls of learning become transparent. Recall the example of Uruguay where due to the COVID pandemic they shifted learning to television to address the inequity of access to the internet and devices. More importantly, it was not a transmission solution but engaged the students in writing and producing the content. One of the most powerful ways to make these new connections and open limitless possibilities is the third element of learning design—leveraging digital.

The combination of access to diverse perspectives and cultures combined with a culture of belongingness and safety is fostering a new curriculum of humanity.

Leveraging Digital is not about focusing on digital tools—devices and software—but rather on the role that interaction with the digital world can play in enhancing Deep Learning. As we saw in Chapter 3, it is about social intelligence developing in relation to machine intelligence. The proliferation of technology, artificial intelligence, and big data permeate all aspects of life. Digital can play an essential role in facilitating Deep Learning partnerships with students, families, community members, and experts regardless of geographical location. It can support student capacity to take control of their own learning both within and outside the classroom walls. Innovations such as ChatGPT offer limitless possibilities. But Driver 2 reminds us we must attend to both Social and Machine Intelligence by ensuring students have the skills and competencies to discern, critically assess, and create new knowledge in innovative ways. They can use digital ubiquitously to engage, motivate, and amplify learning.

In the past, we asked students to solve problems that had already been solved. Today we need students to create and apply their solutions to real-world problems while using the digital world to connect and collaborate locally and on a global scale. Leveraging digital is about increasing social intelligence (especially among students, teachers, parents, and principals working together) that places students on a footing to interact with the power of AI. Leveraging digital is integral to the fourth element of learning design.

Pedagogical Practices bring precision to the question, What is the best way for students to learn? Supporting students to experience deep collaborative learning that extends beyond the classroom walls requires changes in practice. It's about putting a new lens of depth over research-proven pedagogies that remain essential while developing emerging innovative practices. The process begins with knowing the context of students and using culturally grounded pedagogies to ensure students are heard and valued. Becoming *pedagogically relevant* amid diverse cultures, especially with respect to those who have been left out historically, is a deep problem that must be at the forefront of pedagogical development in the immediate next phase.

Teachers who embrace Deep Learning think in terms of creating Deep Learning experiences and richer units of learning that provide time to develop the competencies and often utilize innovative pedagogies and teaching models, such as inquiry learning, problem and project-based learning, and emerging ones like knowledge building platforms. These models most often require the teacher to take on the role of activator and for students to have choice and take responsibility for their learning. The learning experiences may be longer chunks or daily Deep Learning but most often engage students in authentic, relevant problems or simulations where learning is applied in the real world. Most often this combination of choice, more meaningful tasks, and increased student responsibility leads to increased engagement.

These four elements work in combination and give specificity to design and learning.

3. LEARNING CONDITIONS

Deep Learning design and inclusion of the Global Competencies do not happen by chance. There are scores of individual innovative teachers and leaders on the frontier of this work, but for Deep Learning to become part of the "system" supportive conditions and practices need to be in place in schools, districts, and systems and become embedded. The challenge is how to move Deep Learning from a few bright spots of innovation to a pervasive shift in thinking and practices that impact all learners across the entire school and system.

As you think of the vignettes that we provided in Chapters 2–5 you will appreciate how these organizations created systems of supportive conditions. Our third component of the framework consists of three rubrics that identify the conditions and practices needed to support DL: School Learning Conditions, District Learning Conditions, and System/Policy Learning Conditions. We acknowledge that more work needs to be done to develop the structures, cultures, and conditions that will be essential to support the Systemness model that we advocated in Chapter 5. As we said earlier, the whole system has to learn. Toss out bald compliance; form partnerships across the system; make well-being, learning, and the Global Competencies the focus; and by all means measure their progress transparently. We have a hunch that people don't mind open accountability if the right agenda is in play.

SCHOOL LEARNING CONDITIONS

School Learning Conditions are captured in a rubric that can be used by school leaders and leadership teams to collaboratively *assess* current conditions in the school and identify areas of need; *design* a plan to address the identified gaps or needs; *implement* and monitor the plan; and *measure* progress on the condition over time to inform the next cycle of school growth. The same four phases of the collaborative inquiry cycle—assess; design; implement; and measure, reflect, and change—used in classroom learning design are mirrored in this reflective process using the school conditions rubric.

As schools began using Deep Learning more consistently, we observed a new change dynamic emerging from an implementation mindset of rolling out to a more organic process of colearning and codevelopment where all levels learn from the work and adjust plans and strategies. It is crucial to note that learning occurs laterally (within and across schools, districts, and systems) much more so than in traditional hierarchical schooling.

Schools do not operate in a vacuum and are impacted by the policies of districts and systems. But they should not wait for the system to get its act together; in fact, proactive schools contribute to district improvement. The good news is that innovative schools go outside to get better inside. They take advantage of the ideas and resources of the system to make headway, and, as they make progress, begin to influence upward to change policies and structures. They seek connections with other schools in their jurisdiction or virtually to share practices. These intraschool and interschool connections accelerate progress.

DISTRICT LEARNING CONDITIONS

Districts can play a vital role by enabling the conditions that foster a shift to Deep Learning mindsets and practices while removing barriers to promote the spread of best practices across whole systems. *District* denotes the local organization of schools so it may be municipalities (Finland), local networks (New Zealand), or clusters within a state system (Australia).

The District Learning Conditions rubric can be a useful tool to assess, plan, and measure system progress. Districts that are on the move have a *whole system change* mindset, which we define as a transformation in the culture of learning. Districts with this mindset see Deep Learning as a way of rethinking the learning process for all schools. They foster the connection and mutual colearning of the schools with a mindset of *go outside to get better inside*. Second, they embrace change in the culture of the local authority by working on coherence relative to Deep Learning within their own culture, in relation to local schools, and upward with respect to state policy.

Again, the changes in structures, culture, and behavior are substantial in the new model. The vignettes from OCSB (Canada) in Chapter 2, Anaheim Union High School District (California) in Chapter 3, and AISNSW (Australia) and Uruguay in Chapter 5 demonstrate the impact when districts integrate the thinking seamlessly into all decisions in the organization. The changes to the learning process are perceived as connected. Common language and purpose evolve and spread; thus, the change is systemic, not fragmented.

SYSTEM/POLICY LEARNING CONDITIONS

Frankly, system conditions conducive for widespread Deep Learning are not well developed. Our new formulations of system change (Driver 4) stress: build the base (school and community level), mobilize the middle (districts and regions), and intrigue or entice the top (policymakers). Admittedly we are being a bit playful here, but the top has had a challenging time finding its best role in Deep Learning system change. We have several examples at the district level but once it moves beyond the district, only Uruguay among our cases managed to do this well.

The good news is that more of those at the top are showing an active interest in transforming how they do business (Well-Being and Learning). We would say that this is partly a function of good local innovations (as in our cases) becoming more widely known, and partly because the cascade of destructive forces we discussed in Chapter 1 may be finally registering. The need now is to build new systems around the kinds of cases we have offered in this book. Strategies may include policy development, capacity-building opportunities, funding, and accountability. The cases we've provided actively support partnerships with other community groups and find ways to reallocate resources to support the learning work. They integrate the thinking seamlessly into all decisions in the organization.

The three levels of learning conditions (school, district, system) have served to guide, shape, and support Deep Learning in these initial phases. Explicit focus will continue to be placed on these three contextual conditions *as integrated* with the 6Cs and the four elements of the learning design.

The Collaborative Inquiry Process underpins every aspect of the Deep Learning Framework, from designing experiences in classrooms to planning for school development to strategizing ways to move an entire system. As a partnership committed to knowledge building, this process has led us to significant insights about the purpose and practice of Deep Learning in an evolving world.

EMERGING ISSUES AND INSIGHTS

It is not surprising that when you tackle transformational system change in a system that has been stagnant for fifty years, key underlying issues come to the fore. There are four that we identify here: equity-equality, well-being, content or DL, and standardized testing.

EQUALITY, EQUITY, AND WELL-BEING INTERTWINED

Deep Learning tackles issues of equity, equality, and well-being simultaneously. Deep Learning is good for all, but it is especially effective for those most marginalized from schooling because it shifts the learning process to one that is authentic, engaging, and student centered. The deep attention to culture, context, and belonging along with well-being are on everyone's agenda. The growing anxiety and stress of youth and the disengagement with traditional schooling demand a new way of learning.

Deep Learning is good for all, but it is especially effective for those most marginalized from schooling because it shifts the learning process to one that is authentic, engaging, and student centered.

EQUITY-EQUALITY

The issues of social justice and equity are more urgent than ever. Despite huge investments in equity programs, the world has seen little success. We believe that is due to the siloed nature of the solutions. Equality is not a program but must be a lens that we use for every decision and set of strategies that permeate every aspect of learning and living. Jean Clinton, child psychiatrist, describes the impact of Deep Learning on issues of equity this way: "When students fully engage with the 6Cs, those students who come from disadvantage have profound and deeper opportunity to engage in learning because they are able to bring their experiences and life knowledge, rather than being labeled as not having what we need to know" (Clinton, personal communication, 2017).

We are working in California and are engaged in its current focus on community schools. While this massive investment of $4 billion could go wrong and amount to little more than wrap-around services, we are encouraged by some early examples linking learning, well-being, and equity. Anaheim Union High School District (Chapter 3) is an early example of the mindset and integrated approach that is creating pathways for students to excel and connect within their communities and beyond through an intertwined set of community supports, partnerships, and focus on Deep Learning. We are optimistic as well about the ambitious agenda of the San Diego County Office of Education and its forty-two districts (Chapter 4) to significantly reduce poverty and provide the kind of active, engaged learning that will prepare youth to engage in learning and life.

WELL-BEING

Well-being we define as having a sense of purpose, hope, belonging, and meaning that is achieved when our cognitive, emotional, social, and physical needs are being met. Our Deep Learning work is grounded in the fundamentals of neuroscience, promoting connectedness and belonging while working on problems relevant to life circumstances. As noted by our child psychiatrist Jean Clinton, "a focus on the 6Cs immunizes and protects against social and emotional difficulties thus building positive mental health and resilience . . . and levels the playing field for kids from challenging backgrounds" (Quinn et al., 2020, p. 7).

This student-centered, authentic learning attacks the emerging issues of both well-being and equity. We are seeing more and more students from both advantaged and disadvantaged circumstances flourishing. This trio of learning, well-being, and equity holds promise. Stay tuned.

CONTENT OR DEEP LEARNING: THE RAGING DEBATE

Active and engaged learning builds individuals as independent learners who connect to their local communities and are ready to contribute to society. The pandemic has illuminated the fact that a sole focus on academic achievement does not prepare young people for the complex world we now occupy. An emphasis on academic achievement by itself will not be effective in educating students in high poverty, and equally is not serving students of higher socioeconomic status who are struggling with increasing anxiety and stress. As Duncan-Andrade (2022) articulated so powerfully in his recent book *Equality or Equity*,

> The time is long overdue to completely repurpose schools by making student wellness the foundational practice of schools in this nation—youth wellness not as a program, not as an add-on, not as a class, but as the sole purpose. (p. 151)

He elaborates that the four elements of wellness are mind, body, emotion, and spirit. In practice they should be treated as highly intersectional and interdependent. This mirrors the Deep Learning Approach that focuses on *learning partnerships* and *learning environments* as keys to connecting and engaging youth while ensuring they are well. When the content is animated through engagement of the six Global Competencies, the content triggers higher-order thinking and sharpens understanding, reasoning, analysis, and the building of patterns and relationships with other concepts. The knowledge and skills gained stick with learners for life. So, this is not an either/or decision. The new purpose addresses identity and connectedness and uses the Global Competencies as a lens over content to incorporate academic learning. Since Deep Learning focuses on becoming good at learning and good at life, this synergistic development in individuals and in groups creates well-being.

STANDARDIZED TESTING

Let's cut to the chase here. Systems of accountability built into the drivers and Deep Learning are more powerful than standardized tests. We have better learning, better assessments, and better transparency closer to the action as you have seen in the vignettes (see especially the Anaheim case and https://deep-learning.global). And we have better outcome measures. Deep Learning is paving the way by demonstrating how much students are capable of and showing countless examples of how they flourish in Deep Learning environments. As Deep Learning models what is possible, we are encouraged by a few visible signs of a shift from a reliance on standardized testing to valuing multiple forms of assessments. Several examples of robust systems are emerging across member countries, including the Capstone Framework of Anaheim, California (which, as we noted, has formed the basis of a resolution to alter state policy by adding a ninth indicator of success) and the Backpack of Success Skills in Jefferson County, Kentucky. In particular, Anaheim, in partnership with a local technology company, had developed and integrated a new learning platform that ties together pedagogy and their 5Cs through the high school grades, including a culminating capstone graduation performance. They are committed to graduating "socially aware, civic-minded students who are life ready by cultivating the soft and hard skills" (see the vignette in Chapter 3).

There are a growing number of other systems worldwide that are assessing student growth through culminating performances based on competencies. In Australia we are partnering with the Assessment Research Centre at the University of Melbourne to develop new metrics to measure the Global Competencies and provide summative measures for parents and higher education institutions. We cannot wait for the policy level but rather must forge the robust day-to-day Deep Learning examples that will exert vertical influence and propel change.

The Deep Learning Framework is comparatively simple—only three components that bring the new purpose of schooling to life: the 6Cs, the learning design, and the learning conditions—while enabling the assessment of new associated learning outcomes. It is also complex because it comprehensively keeps the focus relentlessly on Well-Being and Learning, embeds strategies to address equity, and mobilizes relationships and the Social and Machine Intelligence to create Systemness.

WHY DEEP LEARNING WORKS

The nature of the Deep Learning tasks is intrinsically motivating for students as they delve into topics that are of real interest to them, have authentic meaning, and are more rigorous. Deep Learning tasks stimulate students to persist and to want to succeed. This combination of autonomy, belongingness, and meaningful work is building capacity in all students, but we have emerging evidence that it is catalytic for success in previously disadvantaged or under-engaged students who are beginning to flourish (see https://deep-learning.global). Our quest is to make Deep Learning the norm for the entire system so that all students thrive.

DEEP LEARNING WORKS BECAUSE IT

1. **Addresses the Whole Child—Whole System**

   Deep Learning develops all aspects of learners, both academic and social-emotional, so that they thrive. It is not a program but a shift in the outcomes of learning and the roles of teachers, leaders, families, and community.

2. **Provides Clarity of Outcomes**

   The Global Competencies (6Cs) provide a comprehensive but clear vision for learning. They serve as a lens to deepen or amplify that learning around selected curriculum goals and are tangible and motivating to use.

3. **Integrates Equity, Well-Being, and Learning**

   Deep Learning intentionally integrates and addresses the needs of youth and adults for equity, well-being, and learning in one coherent approach. The crucial issues of well-being and equality are not add-ons but integral and embedded into this new mindset.

4. **Is Measurable**

   Tools such as learning progressions assess starting points and measure progress in developing proficiency in the competencies. New metrics are in development to provide ways to communicate to parents, higher education, and the business community.

5. **Builds a Common Language and Understanding**

   The *6Cs*, *four elements of learning design*, and *learning conditions* provide a shared language and precision about learning and practice among students, teachers, and families in the design and measurement of learning.

The Deep Learning Framework has been codeveloped with practitioners in countries using a common framework. It has been demonstrated to cross cultures, contexts, and countries with powerful impact in rural or urban areas as well as across advantaged and disadvantaged populations. We are not just reporting on Deep Learning but building and diffusing new knowledge about what works. These five features make the Deep Learning Approach holistic and unique. Examining and improving the world is an essential part of Deep Learning with a strong social connectedness. This connectedness makes it clear that Deep Learning is about improving the humanity paradigm.

GETTING STARTED

There are countless distractors that keep us from this deep transformation. But it is possible to overcome many of these—even during a global pandemic. The Newfoundland

and Labrador English School District (NLESD) serves an entire province across urban, rural, and vast isolated regions. The 256 schools address the needs of all students to experience quality learning while honoring their significant Indigenous populations. Deep Learning was selected as the approach that would prepare their youth for the future in a complex world and bring coherence to the regions. What is truly remarkable is that they began their Deep Learning journey on the same day in March 2020 that much of the world locked down. What is inspiring about this example is that despite a global pandemic they engaged every level and role in their system in this new work. They faced all the same challenges districts across the globe were facing, including health and safety, lockdowns, supply shortages, ambiguity, staff shortages, etc. Rather than be mired in the negative, they took this as an opportunity to create a new culture of learning, embedding the 6Cs into daily Deep Learning. Capacity building was extensive for all roles and amplified when they drew on their rich Indigenous culture to share early examples of success through storytelling. They used a variety of strategies to develop this new learning culture for students and adults alike: diffusion of early innovations, creating spaces to share stories of practice, virtual summits and webinars, a repository for artifacts and examples of impact, and multiple ways to learn and celebrate success.

They intentionally created conditions that fostered collaboration, risk-taking, listening, ownership, voice, and personal meaning. Their journey is captured in two graphics which detail the first 120 days and then the second 120 days (see Figure 6.5). Together, the graphics describe the key decisions that ensured the focus on learning was shared by all and supported even during difficult times.

The NLESD case demonstrates the power of integrating a clear focus on Well-Being and Learning (Driver 1); accelerating the combination of Social and Machine Intelligence by creating strong focused relationships in virtual times (Driver 2); addressing issues of Equity-Equality in their

FIGURE 6.5 ● NLESD: Deep Learning Strategy 2020

Source: Newfoundland and Labrador English School District.

remote communities (Driver 3); and creating a coherent system of supports and sense of Systemness (Driver 4).

We believe that an increase in specific, exciting learning experiences of the kind we have identified and fostered will create a breakthrough. Diffusing Deep Learning is complex work because it depends on building new relationships between and among students, teachers, families, leaders, and community. If these ideas are intriguing and resonate with you, then consider these ten strategies to get started (Gardner et al., 2022).

TEN WAYS TO GET STARTED ON THE DEEP LEARNING JOURNEY

1. **Foster Shared Purpose.** Provide opportunities to explore Deep Learning and how it matters for the changing contexts and futures of the students you serve. Tap into the multitude of videos, vignettes, and webinars at https://deep-learning.global to bring the ideas to life. Have powerful conversations that create a depth of understanding, meaning, and ownership.

2. **Build a Team of Innovators.** Invite those already innovating to influence others using their early experiences. Use rapid cycles of doing and reflecting to adjust strategy and celebrate gains. Go slow to go fast—take time to build trust to support innovation, but don't wait for times to be perfect.

3. **Be Strategic—Set Specific Goals.** Deep Learning can invigorate staff with hope and energy. Access your staff's thinking about ways to begin and supports needed. Establish a small set of goals and get started. Don't wait to get everyone on board but target first steps to get started.

4. **Invest in Capacity Building.** The willingness to innovate is a mix of confidence and competence. Develop competence through frequent opportunities for deep discussion, observations of practice, and time to build skills and knowledge. Create an environment where everyone feels safe to take risks and that they will be recognized for innovating to meet student needs.

5. **Learn From the Work.** Innovation gets you started but it is collaborative reflection that pushes the work forward. Establish a mechanism to consistently learn from practice and apply those insights to next steps. Rapid prototyping of new mindsets and practices about learning will propel results.

6. **Go Outside to Get Better Inside.** No matter how creative and committed teachers are, there is a ceiling to learning if they remain isolated. Create opportunities for sharing within the school through collaborative assessment of student work, examination of learning designs, or capacity building. Accelerate the shift of practices by fostering interschool or interdistrict sharing. Seeing how others are implementing new ideas adds richness and validity.

7. **Manage Distracters.** Sidestep the multiple distracters that keep you from focusing on learning. Instead, focus on how Deep Learning can be a vehicle to achieve school or system priorities. Messaging that makes connections between the priorities and Deep Learning will reduce feelings of being overwhelmed.

8. **Partner With Parents and Community.** Approach parents as partners, finding ways to listen to and respond to their concerns while also engaging them in the new learning practices. When everyone has a voice, commitment accelerates. Link to the expertise beyond the walls of the school or system.

9. **Measure What Matters.** Search out the best examples of innovation and celebrate them often. Don't wait until the end of the journey to take stock and recognize the indicators of early success. If we want new practices to take root, then the spotlight must be on using multiple forms of assessment that allow students to demonstrate their learning.

10. **Join the Movement.** Reach for inspiration, aspiration, and expertise. Everyone is a novice in a new situation, and we need to build on the ideas of innovators before us. As we take our journey and share with and from others, we are enriched, and it is the students who will benefit.

OPTIMISM OR LEARNED HOPEFULNESS

We don't know whether you are optimistic or not. We do know that the problems are severe, that we have a tangible solution emerging, and that we don't have a choice but to go for it. Our optimism is related to the sense that more and more people seem to agree and are willing to join a journey of what we call *learned hopefulness*. We have seen DL work in more and more circumstances. When it comes to DL we have seen people hesitate or doubt at the start, but when DL begins to take hold, especially by the young, that initial hesitancy, that hitch in the step, turns into movement and then a bit of a gallop.

When people are working together in a focused manner on topics that are important to them, they gravitate naturally toward specificity. As noted earlier, we call it specificity without imposition. They're not mandated to change but gravitate to new ideas because they are increasing clarity with experience. It is powerful, and the learning sticks. This collaborative examination of what works and why is pushing the boundaries of how to address issues of equality, equity, and well-being. Teachers share knowledge on how to scaffold experiences and challenges, finely tune them to the needs and interests of students, and maximize learning through relevance, authenticity, and real-world connections. They share a wide repertoire of strategies to meet diverse student needs and interests and a deep understanding of proven models, such as inquiry and problem-based learning. What works with Māori students in New Zealand may be relevant to students in rural Uruguay. There is no one pedagogy—no prescription, but we are building collective knowledge across thousands of classrooms and schools about what engages our humanity. We are building pathways to precision through this collective inquiry and learning more about how this approach is intertwined with the goals of well-being, equity, and equality in varied contexts.

COHERENCE MAKING

Our Deep Learning experiences and the other chapters in this book tell a story. It's a good story that we hope readers can relate to in their own situations. Maybe the connection sparks some to push harder because our stories confirm that they are going in the right direction. Perhaps the revelations stop some in their tracks as they realize that they have been trying to get better at the wrong game. In a complex world, coherence making is always the challenge. Our intention in Deep Learning itself, and in the drivers chapters, is to provide the frameworks, offer case examples for grounded clarity, and provide insights into the various processes. Most of all, we are interested in joint determination of our futures where we learn just as much as anyone, and where we try to equip you with the ideas and tools to cope with destructive problems as we strive to create a viable and flourishing future. A human journey of utmost importance if there ever was one!

Epilogue

The Humanity Paradigm in Action

The reader might well ask at this stage: What is the relationship between the four drivers and the Deep Learning Framework? The drivers serve as a foundation for the Deep Learning (DL) Framework—without which the changes that accrue might be superficial, or not deep enough. Driver 1: Well-Being and Learning is squarely aligned with DL's new purpose. Driver 2: Social and Machine Intelligence buttresses the Global Competencies and the learning design components of DL. Drivers 3 and 4: Equity-Equality Investments and Systemness serve as the system conditions essential to complete the transformation and its impact.

The drivers serve as a foundation for the Deep Learning (DL) Framework—without which the changes that accrue might be superficial, or not deep enough.

What does it mean to be human in 2023? Surely the answer is "very few know," and if they do, they don't know how to get there. Yet, the question for us is: What would a good human do faced with too many choices and too few answers? If you were to think about it in terms of evolution (humans but also other spirits) then the answer might as well be, "That is what evolution is for"—a kind of "don't just stand there, evolve!" Standing by while evolution does its work is no longer good enough. Evolution does not always turn out well, and it's too slow. Andres Campero, a researcher at MIT, suggests that there are three elements at play in human development: genes (evolution), culture, and consciousness. The humanity paradigm contends with all three. It works to influence our future, integrating all three forces. Ask yourself what is vital for our survival, our thriving as a human race. Are trust, compassion, and creativity more likely to be found in a good ten-year-old or in the latest ChatGPT (OpenAI, 2022)?

SIX REFLECTION POINTS

1. Learn from the five innovators (and others like them) that we featured in our vignettes.

2. Choose how you want to live or die.

3. Treat machines as worthy opponents.

4. Keep your eye and heart on the prize; imagine and help create oases of the future.

5. Venture out into system-related partnerships.

6. Just do it: go big and deep; start small, and build steadily for five-plus years.

---

1. LEARN FROM INNOVATORS

The biggest lesson from the five innovators we featured (and there are millions more of them out there) is that they didn't ask for or need permission. You don't need permission for half the things you should want to do. Seek allies for the core, and expand into the future. One of the most impressive features of early innovators is that they seek a much better future than ordinary success. Every time you settle for mere improvement, you undercut deeper change. We already know that systems have a tendency to regress to the norm. This means that partial change is easier to claw back. Go for bigger change (not all at once): a devotion to a humanity paradigm that is fit for the times—eliminating poverty, helping the vast majority thrive. Imagine and formulate lofty plans with others. Co-opt the downtrodden because those closest to the pain have the best ideas as they are liberated for new worthy action.

You don't need permission for half the things you should want to do.

---

2. CHOOSE HOW YOU WANT TO LIVE OR DIE

Passivity is a death warrant. Either choose something worthwhile, or you are in effect finished. We don't know how people thought about the future 2,000 years ago, but we do know that their lives were short (thirty-five years or so) and none too pleasant for the majority. In recent years, the average lifespan in Western countries is about eighty years old. In the poorest countries, it is much lower—more like sixty-five and significantly less if we use "healthy years" as the criterion. For the first time in our lifetimes, average health is deteriorating. Health demographic scientists Wilkinson & Pickett (2019) show that the larger the gaps between the rich and poor, the lower the life expectancy overall. In all scenarios, it is in our self-interest to cultivate and hitch to the right drivers.

We may be perverse, but we think it is a privilege to live in 2023. On good days, the world is magical. It is possible to make it more so—a worthy goal for living. Are we pessimistic? No, just the opposite. The four drivers in action are the shortest possible route between doom and bloom!

3. TREAT MACHINES AS WORTHY OPPONENTS

Speaking of magic, it seems like artificial intelligence (AI) is creating a new world almost every day. It is not out to get humanity—remember, it is not sentient (and yes, that is another story). We should enter the race and ask the big question: How can AI contribute to the fulfillment of the humanity paradigm? Recent developments in AI are astounding in many ways. They can be harnessed to further the human paradigm. Ask this question continually because AI is a continuous and ubiquitous phenomenon.

4. KEEP YOUR EYE AND HEART ON THE PRIZE

We have been around a long time, and never remember a period when so many things have been so unsettled as normal fare for such a seemingly endless time. Unsettled situations allow interventions. Again, we say to be mindful and heartful of the opportunities that such instability brings—opportunities to pursue the humanity paradigm in order to do good for yourself and for others.

5. VENTURE OUT INTO SYSTEM-RELATED PARTNERSHIPS

In Chapter 5, we talked about new system partnerships across the three levels: local, middle, and top (or system). In the next period (2024 onward) we predict that the top (policymakers and politicians) will be open to cooperative endeavors with the other levels. You can't get system transformation without cross-level joint endeavors. We ourselves will be looking for such developments and hope to be directly involved in some of them in the near future. No doubt the drivers will be playing a leading role.

6. JUST DO IT: GO BIG AND DEEP; START SMALL, BUILD STEADILY FOR FIVE+ YEARS

All five of our case examples did just that. Four of the five started at least five years ago, and the fifth, San Diego County, started one year ago and is committed for at least another six years. All are building incrementally and geometrically deeper and wider support as they go.

We are also making progress relative to positioning system change (see Figure E.1).

FIGURE E.1 ● The Solution to System Transformation

| Build the internal system at the local level (school and community) | Strengthen with lateral interaction (across schools and communities) | Develop vertical relationships to government based on partnerships and mutual development | Assess for progress based on precision, not prescription |

Greater focus must be placed on (a) building the internal local systems, (b) enabling local entities to learn from each other, (c) developing two-way vertical learning relationships with governments, and (d) establishing new outcome measures that include well-being and Global Competencies around a spirit of partnership, not compliance.

Our goal has been to provide some ideas and tools that will help the reader navigate an exceedingly complex and unpredictable world. We hope we have provided you with some insights, ideas, and motivation to enter the fray, and for the world to be better off because of it. If there was ever a time to act to save the planet and its inhabitants, it would be now. After ten years of working diligently on changing the system, we have found that transforming the longstanding status quo can be more elusive than we thought. The current structure of schools is not developmentally friendly.

When all is said and done, make sure you have anchored the future (to the best of your ability) with the new purpose: cultivate civic-minded changemakers, embed the four drivers (Well-Being and Learning, Social and Machine Intelligence, Equity-Equality Investments, and Systemness), and ensure that students have developed the 6C competencies essential for life (see also Fullan & Fullan, 2023).

Our book argues that we must change—indeed, transform—the purpose and focus of learning. More than that, we argue that *we must change the way we change!* If you want to change the system deeply, you have to help the whole system to learn how to operate much differently than it has in the past. This means mobilizing the bottom and the middle to interact within and across each other while intriguing the top, all in the interest of emerging system change that serves the humanity paradigm. Be guided by the drivers to go deep. Address the wounds of the pandemic as you develop a new era of education—one that embraces the prosperity of humans and the environment in which we live. There is something profound and heart-warming to realize that our best future will be embracing the humanity paradigm.

References

Bell, A. M., Chetty, R., Jaravel, X., Petkova, N. & Van Reenen, J. (2019). Who becomes an inventor in America? The importance of exposure to innovation. *The Quarterly Journal of Economics*, 134(2), 647–713.

Boushey, H. (2019). *How inequality constrains our economy and what we can do about it*. Harvard University Press.

Brazer, D., & Matsuda, M. (in press). *Education for a purposeful life.* Harvard Education Press.

Breazeal, C. (2019). *Developing social and empathetic AI.* YouTube. World Economic Forum. https://youtu.be/T52g7dCxJ4A

Broussard, M. (2018). *Artificial unintelligence: How computers misunderstand the world.* MIT Press.

Broussard, M. (2023). *More than a glitch: Confronting race, gender, and ability bias in tech.* MIT Press.

Cantor, P., & Osher, D. (2021) *The science of learning and development.* Routledge.

Castaldo, J. (2023, May 1). AI pioneer Geoffrey Hinton leaves Google as he warns of technology's dangers. *The Globe and Mail.* https://www.theglobeandmail.com/business/article-ai -google-godfather-hinton-quits/

Duncan-Andrade, J. (2022). *Equality or equity.* Harvard Education Press.

Eubanks, V. (2017). *Automating inequality: How high tech tools profile, police and punish the poor.* St. Martin's Press.

Foundation for Education Development (2022). *National education consultation report.* https://fed.education/wp-content/ uploads/2022/07/fed-national-consultation-report-2022.pdf

Fullan, J., & Fullan, M. (2023). The convergence of learning and citizenship. *Principal Connections, 26*(3), 4–7.

Fullan, M. (2019). *Nuance: Why some leaders succeed and others fail.* Corwin.

Fullan, M. (2021). *The right drivers for whole system success.* Centre for Strategic Education.

Fullan, M. (2022, September 6). *6 reasons why we should see students as changemakers.* ED Week. https://www.edweek.org/ technology/opinion-here-are-6-reasons-our-students -should-be-seen-as-changemakers/2022/09

Fullan, M. (2023a). *The principal 2.0*. Jossey-Bass.

Fullan, M. (2023b). *Why we can't escape the status quo in education, Part 1; How to address system change education, Part 2*. Ed Week.

Fullan, M., & Edwards, M. (2022). *Spirit work and the science of collaboration*. Corwin.

Fullan, M., & Quinn, J. (2016). *Coherence: The right drivers in action for schools, districts, and systems*. Corwin.

Fullan, M., & Quinn, J. (2020). *How do disruptive innovators prepare today's students to be tomorrow's workforce?: Deep learning: Transforming systems to prepare tomorrow's citizens*. Inter-American Development Bank. http://dx.doi.org/10.18235/0002959

Fullan, M., Quinn, J., & McEachen, J. (2018). *Deep learning: Engage the world change the world*. Corwin.

Fullan, M., Spillane, B., & Fullan, B. (2022). Commentary: Connected autonomy. *Journal of Professional Capital and Community, 7*(4), 329–333.

Fuller, B., & Kim, H. (2022). *Systems thinking to transform schools*. Brookings.

Gardner, M., Quinn, J., Drummy, M., & Fullan, M. (2022, September). *The lowdown on scaling up deep learning across your system*. New Pedagogies for Deep Learning. https://deep-learning.global/wp-content/uploads/2022/10/The-Lowdown-on-Scaling-Up-Deep-Learning.pdf

Goldin, C., & Katz, L. (2008). *The race between education and technology*. Harvard Education Press.

Hannon, V., & Temperley, J. (2022). *FutureSchool: How schools around the world are applying learning design principles for a new era*. Routledge.

Hargreaves, A., & Fullan, M. (2012). *Professional capital: Transforming teaching in every school*. Teachers College Press.

Holmes, W., Bialik, M., & Fadel, C. (2019). *Artificial intelligence in education*. Center for Curriculum Design.

Homer-Dixon, T. (2020). *Commanding hope*. Albert A. Knopf.

Johnson, R. (2022). *Glass onion: A Knives Out mystery*. Netflix.

Kelton, S. (2020). *The deficit myth*. Public Affairs.

Klein, N., & Stefoff, R. (2021). *How to change everything*. Puffin Canada.

Kuhn, T. (1962). *The structure of scientific revolutions*. University of Chicago Press.

Lobel, O. (2022). *The equality machine*. Public Affairs.

Luckin, R. (2018). *Machine learning and human intelligence*. UCL Institute of Education Press.

Malin, H. (2018). *Teaching for purpose*. Harvard University Press.

Markovits, D. (2020). *The meritocracy trap*. Penguin Books.

Mattei, C. (2022). *The capital order*. University of Chicago Press.

Mazzucato, M. (2018). *The values of everything: Making and taking in the global economy.* Hatchett Book Group.

Mazzucato, M. (2021). *Mission economy: A moonshot guide to changing capitalism.* Penguin Press.

Mehta, J., & Datnow, A. (2020). Changing the grammar of schooling. *American Journal of Education, 126,* 1–8.

Milligan, S. (2020). *Future proofing Australian students with new credentials.* University of Melbourne.

Muir, K. (2022). *Putting learners at the centre: Towards a future vision for Scottish education.* Scottish Government.

Northern Alliance. (2022). *Regional improvement collaborative: Phase 4 plan 2022–2025.* https://northernalliance.scot/wp-content/uploads/2022/11/Regional-Improvement-Plan-Phase-4-2022-25.pdf

OpenAI. (2022). "ChatGPT." https://openai.com/blog/chatgpt

Powell, J. A. (2012). Poverty and race through a belongingness lens. *Policy Matters, 1*(5). https://www.coloradotrust.org/wp-content/uploads/2021/10/Poverty_and_Race_through_a_Belonging_Lens-1.pdf

Prensky, M. (2022) *Empowered!: Re-framing 'growing up' for a new age.* Marc Prensky and the Global Ministry of Empowerment, Accomplishment, and Impact.

Putnam, R., & Garrett, S. (2020). *Upswing.* Simon & Schuster.

Quinn, J., McEachen, J., Fullan, M., Gardner, M., & Drummy, M. (2020). *Dive Into deep learning: Tools for engagement.* Corwin.

Raworth, K. (2017). *Doughnut economics.* Chelsea Green Publishing.

Rieble-Aubourg, S., & Viteri, A. (2020). *CIMA brief #20: COVID-19: Are we prepared for online learning?* Inter-American Development Bank. http://dx.doi.org/10.18235/0002303

Sandel, M. (2020). *The tyranny of merit.* Farrar, Straus & Giroux.

Schleicher, A. (2021). *Learning for an interconnected world, COBIS21* [conference link article]. https://consiliumeducation.com/itm/2021/04/28/globally-competent/

Senge, P., & Böll, M. (2023). *Compassion system awareness.* MIT Press.

Statistics Canada. (2021). Ottawa, Ontario. https://www.statcan.gc.ca/

Wallace-Wells, D. (2019). *The uninhabitable earth.* Tim Duggan Books.

Waters, M., & Brighouse, T. (2022). *About our schools: Improving on previous best.* Crown House Publishing.

Wilkinson, R., & Pickett, K. (2019). *Inner level: How more equal societies reduce stress, restore sanity, and improve everyone's well-being.* Penguin Press.

Wilson, E. O. (2017). *The origins of creativity.* W. W. Norton.

Wong, W. (2023, May 2). Putting AI on pause gives us time to regroup around human rights. *The Globe and Mail,* A11.

Index

Acknowledgments

. . . .

We have so many colleagues, friends, and coworkers to thank that it would fill a whole chapter just to list them. Instead, we need to do some grouping. Our central teams—system work and Deep Learning developers—have been fabulous coworkers, codreamers, and close friends in pursuit of better futures. We deeply thank Eleanor Adam, Jean Clinton, Claudia Cuttress, Max Drummy, Bailey Fullan, Josh Fullan, Mary Jean Gallagher, Mag Gardner, Bill Hogarth, and Santiago Rincon-Gallardo. We are very close to practitioners from twenty or so countries in which we work and also learn. They are codevelopers of the ideas, the work, and the impact. In a real sense, they are coauthors of the ideas, and especially the innovations. The leaders from the five case vignettes in this book are standouts: Tom D'Amico and the Ottawa Catholic crowd; Mike Matsuda and his Anaheim band of innovators; Paul Gothold and the San Diego County giant; Jorga Marrum and Chris Morris of the Australia Independent Schools New South Wales contingent; and Miguel Brechner, Leandro Folgar, and Claudia Brovetto of the unstoppable Uruguay system movement that has changed a country for the better. Our system and Deep Learning friends from around the world are too numerous to mention, but we think of them as devoted colleagues in pursuit of transforming learning around the globe.

We thank the Stuart Foundation, which has funded us for a decade in pursuit of system change in California and elsewhere. We could not have done this work without their strong, proactive, relentless support. Our continuing appreciation of Corwin and its team of editors, who made great recommendations and guided us through all stages of the development of the manuscript. Thanks especially to Tanya Ghans, Desirée Bartlett, Heather Kerrigan, and Nyle De Leon.

Special thanks to Trudy Lane for her creative graphics and Kirill A. Egorov for the cover photo that captures the depths of system change.

Then there are the scores of practitioners, including, of course, children of all ages—the best change agents around. All in all, we feel that we are part of a rapidly growing movement to save and enhance the world. Lucky us.

Michael Fullan: All of the above people have made our lives better. For me, I have a sensational stable core led by my wife, Wendy Marshall, and Bailey, Conor and Michelle, Chris, and Maureen and Josh. Living better and living long are, of course, related. I am one lucky man.

Finally, I thank my coauthor, Joanne Quinn, who walked into my office in 1988, when I first became dean at the University of Toronto, and more or less said, "I don't know what you are doing, but let's work together!"

Joanne Quinn: Such a privilege to know our Deep Learning community whose passion, talents, and innovation are a constant energizer! My warmest thanks to my supportive family—especially the newest changemakers, Madison and Malcolm—whose curiosity sparks this work, and the life-long friends and colleagues who inspire me every day.

Finally, a huge thank you to Michael Fullan, who has been an inspiration, a mentor, a coauthor, and a gifted innovator for three decades. It was clear from that first meeting that I didn't want to miss the adventure collaborating!

About the Authors

Michael Fullan, Order of Canada, is the former dean of the Ontario Institute for Studies in Education and professor emeritus of the University of Toronto. He is the coleader of the New Pedagogies for Deep Learning global initiative (www.deep-learning.global).

Michael served as Premier Dalton McGuinty's special policy adviser in Ontario from 2003 to 2013. He received the Order of Canada in December 2012 and holds five honorary doctorates from universities around the world. His interim autobiography, *Surreal Change*, covers his pre–COVID-19 pandemic period to 2018. Michael and his colleagues are now working diligently on field-based comprehensive system change in several countries, under the umbrella of what they call the *humanity paradigm*—equitable-equal deep change that integrates local (school and community), middle (district/regional), and center (policy) entities.

Michael's latest books are *Nuance: Why Some Leaders Succeed and Others Fail* (2019); *Spirit Work and the Science of Collaboration* (with Mark Edwards, 2022); *The Principal 2.0* (2023); and *The Drivers: Transforming Learning for Students, Schools, and Systems* (with Joanne Quinn, 2023).

For more information on books, articles, videos, and podcasts, please go to www.michaelfullan.ca.

An internationally renowned consultant, speaker, and author on learning, leadership, and system change, Joanne Quinn is a passionate voice for reimagining learning that enables all youth to flourish and contribute to the world. As cofounder and global director of New Pedagogies for Deep Learning (NPDL), Joanne leads a global innovation partnership of twenty countries that are collaborating to activate powerful, student-centered, real-world learning by fostering six Global Competencies. The comprehensive approach supports schools, districts, municipalities, and systems to shift practice and impact well-being and equity. As a leader at all levels of education in districts, the Ministry of Education, and the University of Toronto, Joanne has led Whole System Change projects that build the collective capacity of organizations. She continues to consult with governments, school systems, foundations, and policymakers across the globe.

Recent publications include *Coherence: The Right Drivers in Action for Schools, Districts, and Systems* (2016); *Deep Learning: Engage the World Change the World* (2018); *Dive Into Deep Learning: Tools for Engagement* (2020); *Education Reimagined: The Future of Learning* (2020); and *The Drivers: Transforming Learning for Students, Schools, and Systems* (with Michael Fullan, 2023).

A Sage Company

CORWIN HAS ONE MISSION: to enhance education through intentional professional learning.

We build long-term relationships with our authors, educators, clients, and associations who partner with us to develop and continuously improve the best evidence-based practices that establish and support lifelong learning.

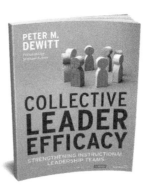

Complement your learning journey with **free resources from Corwin!**

WEBINARS

Listen and interact with education excerpts for an hour of professional learning to gain practical tools and evidence-based strategies—and maybe win some free books!

LEADERS COACHING LEADERS PODCAST

Join Peter DeWitt and his guests as they discuss evidence-based approaches for tackling pressing topics like equity, SEL, burnout, assessment, interrupted formal learning, school administration, and more.

CORWIN CONNECT

Read and engage with us on our blog about the latest in education and professional development.

SAMPLE CONTENT

Did you know you can download sample content from almost every Corwin book on our website? Go to corwin.com/resources for tools you and your staff can use right away!

CORWIN